EDITOR: MARTIN WIND W9-AWR-089

OSPREY
MILITARY

ELITE SERIES

1

THE PARAS
1940-1984

Text by
GREGOR FERGUSON
Colour plates by
KEVIN LYLES

First published in Great Britain in 1984 by
Osprey, an imprint of Reed Consumer Books Ltd.
Michelin House, 81 Fulham Road,
London SW3 6RB
and Auckland, Melbourne, Singapore and Toronto

British Library Cataloguing in Publication Data

Ferguson, Gregor
    The Paras.—(Osprey Elite series; 1)
    1. Great Britain. *Army. Parachute Regiment*—History
    I. Title
    356′.166′0941   UA652.P3

ISBN 0-85045-573-1

Filmset in Great Britain
Printed through World Print Ltd, Hong Kong

Errata:

Plate B3: The SMG should have a straight box
magazine; the shoulder title should be conventional
—the glider badge was not added until 1950.
Plate D1: The Sam Browne with whistle dates from
Maj.Cain's service with the Royal Northumberland
Fusiliers. Plate E25: White and black are reversed.

Acknowledgements

The author wishes to acknowledge with thanks the help
given by the following during the preparation of this
book:
The Commanding Officer, 10th (Volunteer) Battalion
The Parachute Regiment; Major G. G. Norton, Curator,
The Airborne Forces Museum, Aldershot, and Mr. Tom
Fitch, Assistant Curator; No. 1 Parachute Training
School, RAF Brize Norton; General Sir John Hackett;
and finally, 'Peanuts', 'Caz', 'Barney Rubble', and 'the
Int'—they know who they are! Thanks also to my wife,
Cecile, for her patience.

The Sons of Bellerophon

British Airborne Forces came into being on 22 June 1940. On that day the Prime Minister sent a memorandum to Gen. Sir Hastings Ismay, head of the Military Wing of the War Cabinet Secretariat. Mr. Churchill's memo stated flatly that 'We should have a corps of at least five thousand parachute troops . . . Pray let me have a note on the subject'.

Shortly before this date, the Air Ministry had set up an Airborne Forces training school at Manchester's Ringway Airport, where special units and secret agents would be instructed in the art of parachuting by the Royal Air Force. It was to Ringway, on 24 June 1940, that Maj. John Rock, RE, was posted to 'take charge of the military organisation of British Airborne Forces'. He was given no further information as to policy or mission; he had no men, no aircraft, and had never seen a parachute in his life. However, this energetic and imaginative officer set about solving the problems in a logical order, with immensely valuable help from the Central Landing School's commanding officer, Sqn. Ldr. L. A. Strange, DSO, MC, DFC, and from the instructors and parachute packers drafted in from the RAF's parachute training establishment at Henlow. Despite the RAF's desperate shortage of aircraft, six obsolescent Armstrong-Whitworth Whitley bombers were made available. With the arrival of a supply of modified Irvin aircrew parachutes, development work could begin.

It had been decided that some of the newly formed Commando units should be parachute-trained; so No. 2 Cdo., raised only weeks beforehand, duly appeared at Ringway; and the first parachute descent by a British soldier took place—*absit omen!*—on 13 July 1940.

At that time the hideous 'pull-off' method of leaving the aircraft was in vogue. The tail turret of the Whitley was replaced by a kind of open pulpit, on which the victim stood, facing forwards and clutching a handrail. His ripcord was pulled for him by the despatcher, and the deploying parachute yanked him off into space—an appalling experience. Later the Whitley's small ventral turret would be removed so that men could jump through the three-foot hole left in the fuselage floor; the 'chutes had by now been modified for static line operation, i.e. they were linked to the aircraft structure by a strap which automatically opened the pack as the man jumped.

The equipment was by no means perfect at this stage, however; and on 25 July Dvr. Evans, RASC, died when his 'chute 'Roman candled' (failed to deploy). This, and several other potentially disastrous incidents connected with the Whitley, led Maj. Rock to forbid further jumps. The parachute problem was solved by two men: Sir Raymond Quilter and Mr James Gregory, founders of the GQ Parachute Company, who before the war had developed a practicable static-line-operated rig called the 'Statichute'. Unlike the Irvin aircrew model, in which the canopy opened first and then pulled the rigging lines from their stowage to give a very fast but rather robust opening, the GQ model allowed the restrained canopy and the lines to pay out completely before the canopy opened; this gave a smooth, reliable and relatively shock-free opening, more appropriate for a soldier who had to be fit to fight when he landed.

A combination of the Irvin canopy and harness and the GQ deployment method produced one of the best parachutes the world has seen: the X-Type. Surpassed in reliability only by its successor, the PX1, the X-Type had a silk or rayon canopy of 28-foot diameter, the 28 rigging lines uniting in four 'lift webs' which were an integral part of the secure, comfortable harness; a 22-in. central vent reduced oscillation. There remained only one problem: if the canopy was even slightly damp, it would open only

The X-Type parachute demonstrated by a Parachute Regt. captain and an RAF flight sergeant PJI. The outer bag remains attached to the parachute harness. The inner bag, held here by the officer, is released, and the rigging lines pay out from it. The parachute canopy comes free of the inner bag last of all; its apex is attached to the end of the static line by a nylon tie, which breaks under strain, leaving the static line (at the officer's feet) and the inner bag attached to the aircraft anchorage. (ABF Museum)

slowly—if at all . . . This usually fatal malfunction has been greatly reduced, but not entirely eliminated, since the adoption of nylon for canopies.

No 'reserves' were used in those early days—or indeed, until well after the Second World War. The hole in the Whitley's floor was too small to allow a chest-mounted reserve, anyway; and at £60 apiece, reserve 'chutes were probably considered an expensive luxury.

Interspersed with their parachute training, the men of No. 2 Cdo. carried out a gruelling advanced infantry course, similar to the Commando course later set up at Achnacarry Castle; and this formed the basis for selection and training of volunteers to the new Airborne arm. During the summer and autumn of 1940 the unit carried out several exercises and demonstrations for the 'brass', but saw no action. On 21 November the unit was re-named '11 Special Air Service Battalion'; strengthened by an influx of volunteers, it was now officially divided into a parachute and a glider wing. Of course, there were no gliders . . .

An order had in fact been placed with the General Aircraft Company for 400 ten-man Hotspur gliders, similar in general capability to the German DFS-230. Other types under consideration were the 25-man Horsa; an intermediate 15-man type, which never saw the light of day; and the giant Hamilcar, which would carry light tanks. Glider pilots were recruited and trained both by the RAF and the Army: the former taught them to fly, and the latter, to fight—for the crews of these 'one-way-trip' aircraft would have to take their place beside the infantry after landing. This concept would be regularised with the formation, in December 1941, of the Glider Pilot Regiment.

Besides the problem of getting men out of the aircraft and on to the ground safely, Rock and Strange were faced with the question of how they should carry their weapons, if at all. At this primitive stage in the development of military parachuting it was considered enough just to get the man down in one piece: his equipment would have to follow. It did so in a variety of containers based more or less upon the RAF 'bombcell' supply container, a device which could be dropped either from a bomb-bay or from external racks. The several designs and sizes included one square container built to take radio sets. The developed versions of the 'bombcell' were called 'CLE Containers', after Ringway's new name: the Central Landing Establishment.

In retrospect, it seems that more time might profitably have been spent on confronting the vital problem of how long it was going to take an unarmed man, stumbling around a rough DZ at night, to find his weapon; and rather less upon the special clothing developed for him to wear while he did the stumbling. Over his ordinary battledress and web equipment, the early parachutist wore the grey-green cotton Jacket, Parachutist—a long-sleeved garment which fastened between the legs by means of press-studs, and which was clearly modelled on the German smock. It presented a smooth outline to the slipstream, and was thought to reduce the chances of a rigging line fouling the personal equipment. Other German-inspired devices tested but not persevered with were side-lacing, crepe-soled boots, and knee and elbow pads; it was found in practice that the standard 'ammunition boot' and a properly executed landing-roll were perfectly adequate protection for men who did not have the handicap of the badly-designed German parachute harness (see Men-at-Arms 139, *German Airborne Troops 1939–45*). The leather flying helmet worn by the first, and most courageous parachutists was soon replaced by a canvas affair with thick chunks of sorbo rubber padding—a comfortable headgear, seen in use until the late 1950s. The first type of steel helmet introduced for airborne wear had a hard, black rubber rim; this did not last long, before the classic rimless type appeared.

European Operations 1941–42

The Tragino Aqueduct Raid

The men of 11 SAS Bn. had joined up to see some action, and by the end of 1940 some were getting so bored with development work—vital as it was—that they were requesting transfers back to their old units. In early January 1941 these requests ceased: a rumour ran around Ringway, to the effect that something was in the wind. The commanding officer, Lt. Col. C. I. A. Jackson, paraded his men and called for volunteers for a 'deep penetration' raid behind enemy lines. Every man present volunteered; and in due course seven officers and 31 men were selected to form 'X Troop, 11 SAS' for Operation 'Colossus'. The target was the Tragino Aqueduct in Italy. It was reasoned that if this could be destroyed much of southern Italy would be

Sergeant parachutist demonstrating the 'LMG valise' in which the Bren gun was carried on the jump. It was obviously vital for the parachutist to 'get rid of' the heavy valise as soon as his canopy opened—to land with it strapped in this position would probably be fatal. Just visible at the front of the valise are quick-release pins securing the straps around neck and leg, joined by a line. In his right hand the sergeant holds the canvas friction device by which he lowered the valise on its 20 ft rope; the rope's attachment to the right hand side of his harness is just visible below his right elbow. (ABF Museum)

The Denison smock, introduced in 1942. This early version has the half-length zip, storm cuffs, and buttoning tightening-tabs at the sides of the skirt. Many soldiers sewed the tops of woollen socks to the cuffs to make them windproof. The basic colour was mid-green, with a random overprint of dark green and brown patches.

denied water for some considerable time. This would hamper the war effort of the enemy whom British troops were fighting in North Africa, and would cause 'alarm and despondency' among the Italians. While this may have been the ostensible rationale, the real aim was, of course, to see what airborne troops were made of; perfectly aware of this, the men of X Troop trained hard at Tatton Park, Ringway's training DZ, where a full-scale model of the aqueduct was built.

On the night of 7 February 1941 X Troop, commanded by Maj. T. A. G. Pritchard, took off from Mildenhall in Suffolk for an epic flight across occupied France in six Whitley bombers of No. 91 Sqn. RAF, led by Wg. Cdr. J. B. Tate. In Malta final plans were laid for the submarine HMS *Triumph* to lie off the mouth of the River Sele to pick up the troops after the raid. Emplaning on Malta at dusk on 10 February, the paratroopers arrived over their DZ only 12 minutes late. Unfortunately, one aircraft went astray and dropped its stick some distance away; this party—inevitably—consisted of the sappers who were to actually blow the aqueduct, under the command of Capt. G. F. K. Daly, RE. Moreover, icing caused two of the explosives containers to 'hang up'. Since Pritchard still had some 1,000lbs. of assorted charges he

decided to press on. A covering party kept watch while the senior surviving sapper, 2nd Lt. A. Patterson, RE, placed explosives on the aqueduct. Meanwhile Lt. Tony Deane-Drummond had discovered a wooden bridge not far away, and this was also mined. Both charges exploded almost simultaneously.

Mission accomplished—after a fashion; now came the problem of getting home. The submarine lay some 50 mountainous miles to the west; with four days and nights to make the journey, the paratroopers formed into three parties and began to make their separate ways to the rendezvous. All were spotted by civilians, and captured. The sappers from the missing stick were taken prisoner after trying to bluff a village mayor into providing them with transport! Even if they had succeeded in evading the Italians, there would have been a bitter disappointment waiting—the submarine had been compromised by an aircraft crash-landing nearby, and it had been decided to leave the parachutists to their fate rather than risk the submarine.

Although the effect on the Italian war effort was minimal, the effect on Italian morale of this landing in the heart of their country was considerable. It was also a valuable achievement for the parachutists to have proved themselves in action, even on so small a scale, at a time when Britain was reeling from defeat to defeat. Many of X Troop were to escape—among them Tony Deane-Drummond, who would be captured again at Arnhem, and would again escape.

Unit organisation

After this heartening success an expansion of Airborne Forces was ordered; and in September 1941, 1st Parachute Brigade was formed under Lt. Col. (soon, Brig.) Richard Nelson Gale, MC, who was given a free hand to select his officers.

On 15 September, 11 SAS Bn. became 1st Parachute Bn., under Lt. Col. E. E. 'Dracula' Down. The 2nd Para Bn., under Lt. Col. E. W. C. Flavell, MC, included a Scottish C Coy., commanded first by Maj. P. Teichman and later by Maj. John Dutton Frost, a Regular from The Cameronians (Scottish Rifles). The 3rd Para Bn. was commanded by Lt. Col. G. W. Lathbury, MBE. The battalions were distinguished by lanyards in green (1st), yellow (2nd) and red (3rd), and Bde.

HQ wore blue lanyards. Officers and men wore the uniforms and headgear of their parent regiments—there was no direct entry into the Airborne Forces at this time.

On 10 October 1941 the 31st Independent Brigade Group (recently returned, mountain-trained, from India) was renamed 1st Air-Landing Bde. Gp.; and in December the Glider Pilot Regiment was formed to provide the officers and NCOs who would fly the Air-Landing troops into battle. All airborne troops were volunteers, though not always, perhaps, in the very strictest sense of the word. Many glider troops 'were volunteered' for this duty (transitive verb!), but they could transfer out if they wished. Few did so; and the later combat records of these units speak for themselves.

The Bruneval Raid

On 27 February 1942 the second major action fought by Airborne Forces took place: a parachute raid on a German radar site outside Bruneval, a village on the northern coast of France near Le Havre. The operation was proposed by Adm. Lord Louis Mountbatten, Chief of Combined Operations, and C Coy., 2nd Para Bn. was trained for the task. The plan was for a company group of parachutists to attack and dismantle as much of the radar equipment as possible, before being extracted—with such parts as they could carry—by the Royal Navy under RAF fighter cover.

Operation 'Biting', this first true combined operation, was a complete success. Maj. John Frost led his men in the drop from Whitleys of No. 51 Sqn. RAF, and carried out the assault with great precision. The 1st Para Fd. Sqn. RE, under Capt. Denis Vernon, assisted an RAF radar technician, Flt. Sgt. E. W. F. Cox, to dismantle what he could and photograph the rest, all under heavy and accurate enemy fire. The force withdrew with their booty and prisoners to a beach below the coastal cliffs, where they fought off a determined enemy counter-attack before being taken off in the nick of time by naval landing craft. What could have been a major problem worked to Frost's advantage: two sticks under Lt. Euen Charteris had been dropped a mile from the DZ, on the far side of the village. Charteris led his men through the village, fighting a brisk action on the way, and attacked the German pillbox covering the embarkation beach from the rear.

This major mistake, though it had no serious consequences on this occasion, highlighted a problem inherent in airborne operations: getting the paratroops to the right place at the right time. It was no use simply drafting in aircrews for operations on an *ad hoc* basis; trained specialists were needed, and to this end, just before the Bruneval raid, No. 38

North Africa, where the Parachute Regt. earned nine of its 28 World War II battle-honours. Tamera, the site of one of their hardest engagements, lies between Sedjenane and 'Beggar's Bump'.

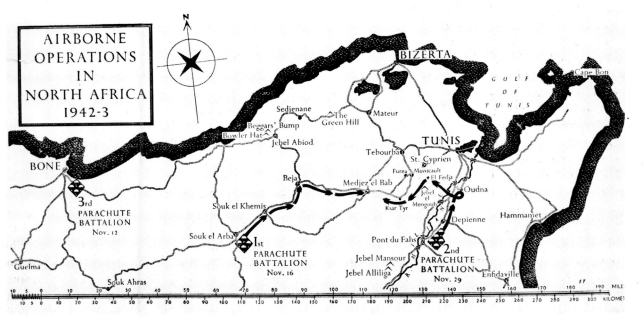

Rear view of fully equipped paratrooper, 1944; he is armed with the standard infantry weapon, the .303in. Lee-Enfield rifle No. 4, and has a 2-in. mortar tucked under the flap of his small pack. Note camouflage face veil worn over the shoulders, and toggle rope—a simple and versatile piece of kit. (Imp.War Museum)

Wing, Army Co-operation Command, RAF was formed on 15 January 1942 under Gp. Capt. Sir Nigel Norman, Bt. While the troops were engaged in training over the next few months, Norman sent his aircrews on raids over Occupied Europe to give them practice in navigation and combat flying. The pilots and crews of No. 38 Gp. became something of an élite within the RAF.

1st Airborne Division

Following a stiff memo from Churchill to Gen. Ismay in the wake of the German airborne invasion of Crete in May 1941, the War Office had begun to take Airborne Forces seriously. A Guards officer, Brig. F. A. M. 'Boy' Browning, was promoted major-general and made GOC Paratroops and Airborne Troops. In October 1941 he was ordered to raise a complete airborne division. He took to this task with a will, since he was a great believer in the new arm, and knew that if they were to play a major part in any battle the paratroops must not be deployed in 'penny packets'. He pressed for an orthodox divisional structure whose equipment scales reflected the airborne rôle, and which would be committed to battle as a whole. Although he encountered stubborn opposition in both the War Office and Air Ministry, Browning had the 'clout' without which very little can be quickly accomplished in the British forces. He used it to good effect, and has often been called the 'father' of British Airborne Forces—though 'guardian' would be more apt, since the conception, after all, was Churchill's.

Mid-1942 saw the 1st Parachute Bde. formed and ready for action, and the 2nd being raised. This was formed round the nucleus of the 4th Para Bn., under Lt. Col. M. R. J. Hope-Thompson, MC, MBE. The other units were the 5th (Scottish) Para Bn.—formerly, 7th Bn., The Queen's Own Cameron Highlanders—under Lt. Col. A. Dunlop; and 6th (Royal Welch) Para Bn.—formerly, 10th Bn., The Royal Welch Fusiliers. The 5th wore the Balmoral bonnet instead of the red beret, with Army Air Corps cap badges on patches of Hunting Stewart tartan; the 6th retained the black collar ribbons of the Royal Welch Fusiliers. The 4th Bn. adopted a black lanyard, and the practical habit of painting all webbing equipment black—a privilege withdrawn for no apparent reason in 1946.

In April 1942 the Airborne Forces Depot was established at Hardwick Hall. On 1 August the battalions, which had until this date been part of no parent regiment or corps, were formed into The Parachute Regiment as part of the newly created Army Air Corps. Browning decided that the Corps should have some distinctive form of headgear, and he chose the beret as being most practical for parachutists. An orderly was paraded at Wellington Barracks in London to model different shades of red, blue and green. The assembled 'brass' could not make up their minds between maroon and blue, so the orderly's opinion was sought; he chose the maroon, and his preference was endorsed by Gen. Sir Alan Brooke, Chief of the Imperial General Staff. At the same time the famous Airborne flash—Bellerophon, the first airborne warrior, astride the winged horse Pegasus—was designed by Edward Seago, camouflage officer of Southern Command.

Its colours, and those of the Airborne arm-of-service strip worn below the patch on each sleeve of the battledress blouse, were Cambridge blue and claret. These were Browning's pre-war racing colours; they were not chosen, as has been suggested, by his wife, the novelist Daphne du Maurier.

When formed in December 1941 the Glider Pilot Regiment came under the command of Maj. (later Lt. Col.) George Chatterton, DSO, a former RAF fighter pilot. His standards were high: barely a tenth of the volunteers actually qualified for their Army Air Corps wings, worn on the left breast of the Denison smock or BD blouse.

Operation 'Freshman'

On 19 November 1942 the first glider-borne assault undertaken by British Airborne Forces took place. This was an assault by 30 sappers of 9 Fd. Coy. (Airborne) RE and 261 Fd. Pk. Coy. (Airborne) RE, led by Lts. A. C. Allen and D. A. Methuen, RE, on the German Norsk Hydro heavy water plant near Vermork, some 60 miles west of Oslo in Norway. The two gliders were flown by Sgts. M. F. C. Strathdee and P. Doig of the Glider Pilot Regt., and Plt. Off. Davis and Sgt. Fraser of the RAAF. The Halifax bomber glider-tugs were commanded by Gp. Capt. T. B. Cooper of No. 38 Wing, RAF.

They took off shortly after nightfall from Skitten aerodrome in northern Scotland. Of the small force sent out, only one Halifax returned. The second bomber crashed in appalling weather, while both gliders made heavy crash landings which killed many of the passengers. The survivors were interrogated by the Gestapo, and subsequently murdered in accordance with Hitler's notorious 'Commando Order' to shoot all saboteurs and commandos. Their fate was only discovered at the end of the war when 1st Airborne Div. arrived in Norway. This gallant, tragic, and some would say ill-conceived venture at least proved that gliders could be towed 400 miles across the sea to a target and—weather permitting—get their passengers on to the ground. The Norsk Hydro plant was later destroyed by Norwegian patriots, immortalised in the fictionalised film '*The Heroes of Telemark*'.

Operation 'Freshman' was also a 'first' in its use of an air-ground radio beacon coded 'Rebecca-Eureka'. 'Rebecca' was a homing receiver installed in the aircraft; 'Eureka' was the transmitter set up on the LZ—in this case it had been smuggled into Norway some time previously. The system broke down on this first occasion, but later functioned well, manned by the pathfinders of both British airborne divisions in Sicily, Normandy, Holland and at the Rhine crossings.

The Mediterranean 1942–45

North Africa: 'Die Röte Teufeln'

On 8 November 1942 the Allies invaded Algeria and Morocco: an operation which was intended, first, to cut off Rommel's supply lines from Europe, and subsequently to destroy the Axis forces in North Africa between two enemies. The 1st Para Bde. was detached from 1st Airborne Div., and placed for this campaign under the command of the Allied 1st Army. By now Gale had left the brigade to become Director of Air at the War Office, and Flavell had taken over command. Frost had succeeded Flavell in command of 2nd Para Bn., and 'Dracula' Down had left 1st Para Bn. to take over 2nd Para Bde.; Lt. Col. S. J. L. Hill now commanded 1st Para Bn., and Lt. Col. R. G. Pine-Coffin led 3rd Para Bn. after Lathbury's departure for the War Office.

During the summer all three units had benefited greatly from pooling their experience with the US 82nd Airborne Div., which had arrived in the UK earlier in the year. Among the equipment the Americans brought with them were the C-47 Skytrain (the military transport version of the DC-3 Dakota); its specialised C-53 Skytrooper paratroop model; and the ubiquitous jeep. The C-53 was found to be the ideal aircraft for parachuting, with its high payload and large fuselage door; while the jeep was found to fit neatly into the Horsa glider, after a minor modification to the aircraft.

While the 2nd Para Bde. had been forming in England and the 1st was preparing for action, two more brigades were being raised: the 3rd, which would form part of the 6th Airborne Div. (of whom, and their commander, Maj. Gen. Richard Gale, more anon); and the 4th, which trained at RAF Ramat David in Palestine. Earmarked for service with 1st Airborne Div., 4th Para Bde. comprised 10th Para Bn. under Lt. Col. K. B. I. Smyth (formed from 2nd Bn. The Royal Sussex Regt.);

and 156th Para Bn. under Lt. Col. Sir Richard des Voeux (which had originally been formed as 151st Para Bn. from volunteers in India). The 4th Bde.'s third unit was to be 11th Para Bn., formed early in 1943 around a cadre from 156th Para Battalion. The brigade commander, from then until its destruction at Arnhem, would be Brig. J. W. 'Shan' Hackett, a Regular cavalry officer.

The first operation carried out by a complete unit of 1st Airborne Div. was a parachute assault on the vital airfield at Bône on the North African coast about halfway between Algiers and Tunis. The 3rd Para Bn. (less A Coy., for whom there were insufficient aircraft) flew from St. Eval in Cornwall to Algiers/Maison Blanche via Gibraltar. They emplaned for their first taste of action on the morning of 12 November 1942. The drop went in at 0830 hrs., and the battalion was put down very accurately by the crews of the USAAF's 60th Group. They were observed while in the air by a force of German Junkers Ju52/3m transports who were carrying Luftwaffe paratroopers towards the same objective: on seeing that they had lost the race, they turned back. The airfield was deserted, and 3 Para were reinforced that same day by No. 6 (Army) Commando and a squadron of RAF Spitfires.

The next day the rest of 1st Para Bde. disembarked at Algiers after a not uneventful sea voyage. In winter rains, the other two battalions were soon in action. The 1st Para Bn. was ordered to take a vital road junction near Beja, 90 miles west of Tunis, and to try to turn the local French forces against the Germans. Lacking proper intelligence, maps and aerial photos, Hill decided to lead his battalion from the front. On 15 November they flew from Maison Blanche; on arrival over the objective Hill spotted what looked like a good DZ, and he and his stick jumped—this being the signal for the battalion to follow. Their reception was friendly, and the CO decided to push on—in commandeered buses—for Beja and, subsequently, Mateur. There a brisk and successful action against a German armoured column convinced any wavering Frenchmen that the Allied invasion was a good thing. In a later attack on an Italian tank position near Sidi N'Sir the CO was wounded, and replaced by Maj. Alistair Pearson. By 10 December 3 Para was confident enough to fight off (supported by a

squadron from 17th/21st Lancers and 2nd Bn., The Lancashire Fusiliers) a battalion-sized German attack, and to rout the enemy with a bayonet charge.

The 2nd Bn., under Johnny Frost, had meanwhile carried out an ill-conceived and useless operation against airfields near Depienne, some 30 miles south of Tunis. When the battalion jumped on 29 November it was again a case of the CO having to pick his own DZ. The airfield had been abandoned for some time, so Frost led his men some ten miles on foot to Oudna, where A Coy. took the airfield. An armoured thrust was supposed to begin that day, to link up with the paratroopers. Since there were no enemy aircraft left at Oudna to be destroyed, Frost decided to withdraw westwards to meet up with the tanks. However, the armour was held up by the unexpected level of enemy resistance; and Frost was informed by radio that he had been virtually written off, 50 miles behind enemy lines.

The 2nd Para Bn.'s retreat from Oudna, which owed much to Frost's leadership, was a heroic march. Under constant attack from Germans guided by the hostile Tunisian Arabs, the unit finally made it to Medjez el Bab—after losing 16 officers and 250 men. This action, like so many others in the history of The Parachute Regiment, inspired poetry. Richard Spender of the 2nd Bn. was to write of that march in words which might equally have applied—40 years later—to the action of 2 Para at Goose Green, or 3 Para on the slopes of Mt. Longdon:

> 'And, with the night, perhaps some God looking down
> With dull, cold eyes, by the near stars, will see
> One lonely, grim battalion cut its way
> Through agony and death to fame's high crown.'

On 8 February 1943 the whole 1st Para Bde. took up a position in the front line, where they would fight as infantry for the rest of the Tunisian campaign. In the worst possible weather conditions the paratroopers fought with great gallantry: first at Bou Arada, and then in two stiff actions at Tamera, where they earned the unstinting admiration of the German paratroopers who faced them, and the nickname 'Die Röte Teufeln'—the Red Devils. Nearly half of the regiment's battle-honours were

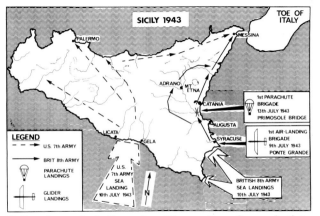

SICILY 1943

TOE OF ITALY

PALERMO

MESSINA

ADRANO MT. ETNA

CATANIA

AUGUSTA

LICATA GELA

SYRACUSE

1st PARACHUTE BRIGADE
13th JULY 1943
PRIMOSOLE BRIDGE

1st AIR-LANDING BRIGADE
9th JULY 1943
PONTE GRANDE

U.S. 7th ARMY SEA LANDING 10th JULY 1943

BRITISH 8th ARMY SEA LANDINGS 10th JULY 1943

Sicily: the scale is deceptive. The scatter of parachutists extended from the Primosole Bridge DZ as far as Adrano and Mt. Etna some 30 miles away.

earned between November 1942 and April 1943. In that time they killed or wounded some 5,000 of the enemy; captured another 3,500; and received a record number of gallantry decorations for a formation going into action for the first time.

Sicily: Operations 'Fustian' and 'Marston'

In June 1943 the 1st Para Bde. was joined by the 2nd Bde., the 4th Bde. minus 11th Para Bn., and the 1st Air-Landing Brigade. The complete 1st Airborne Div. was assembled near Oran for the invasion of Sicily: under the command of Montgomery's 8th Army, they were assigned key bridges and other features as objectives along the axis of Monty's advance up the east coast of Sicily towards Mt. Etna and Messina.

They trained hard, not for their own benefit alone, but also for that of the brave, willing, but rather inexperienced aircrews of the USAAF 60th Group who would fly some of them into battle. The seaborne landings were scheduled for 10 July, so the first airborne operation—Operation 'Fustian'—was planned for the night of the 9th/10th. This gave little time for preparation, especially by the British glider pilots, many of whom would be flying the unfamiliar American WACO CG-4 into action for the first time. 1st Airborne's divisional commander, Maj. Gen. G. F. Hopkinson, had enthused Montgomery with the possibilities of using airborne troops. This enthusiasm was not shared by 'Boy' Browning, who had been arguing with the commander of the US 82nd Airborne Div.—who would go into action at the same time—over the allocation of the (mainly American) aircraft

available. Browning backed up Hopkinson, with some reluctance; Chatterton, of the Glider Pilot Regt., did the same, with even greater reluctance.

The targets allocated to the British airborne division were the Primosole Bridge south of Catania (1st Para Bde.); and the Ponte Grande north of Syracuse (1st Air-Landing Bde.); as the latter was closest to the advancing 8th Army it would be the glider troops who went into action first—their baptism of fire. With only 129 WACO and eight Horsa gliders available, it was decided to take all possible heavy weapons and engineer support, making room by leaving one battalion behind. The unlucky unit (or lucky—it depended upon the point of view) was 1st Bn., The Royal Ulster Rifles.

Towed by 109 C-47s of the USAAF's 51st Wing, and seven Halifaxes and 21 Albermarles of the RAF's No. 38 Wing, the gliders left Kairouan shortly before 1900 hrs. on 9 July. They flew first to Malta, where they turned straight for the coast of Sicily. Due to offshore winds, poor visibility, and the fire of nervous Royal Navy guncrews, more than

Southern Italy, October 1944: preparing a CLE container for the drop on Megara airfield, Athens. This particular container carries several wicker baskets filled with what look like medical supplies. Note the shock-absorbing structure at the end of the container, by the soldier's left knee; and the wicker panniers in the background. (ABF Museum)

The Megara drop. The wind across the DZ was nearly 30 knots, and there were many casualties. The lowest paratrooper, with his knees drawn up, is about to hit the earth painfully. The topmost man is spilling air from the wrong side of his canopy, adding a further eight knots to his ground speed! (Imp.War Museum)

half the gliders landed in the sea.

The brigade commander, Brig. P. H. W. Hicks, was one of the unlucky ones. As they clambered on to the wing of their rapidly sinking glider he muttered to his brigade major, 'All is not well, Bill!' Together with their pilot (Chatterton himself, who had never been madly in love with the plan, anyway) they swam ashore with the rest of the passengers; and after a number of adventures they managed to reach their headquarters. They were luckier than many of the men who fell into the sea that evening.

Only one glider carrying a single platoon of the 2nd Bn., The South Staffordshire Regt. had landed on the correct LZ. Lt. Withers led a small force across the river to attack the far end of the Ponte Grande; they succeeded, and, as stragglers gathered around them, they began a desperate defence of the bridge against enemy counter-attacks. With never more than 90 men, they held out until about 1500 hrs. on the afternoon of the 10th, when the last 15 or

so men were overrun by the Germans. Just an hour later the advance elements of the ground forces arrived and re-took the objective.

The rest of the fragmented brigade fought a number of lesser actions which led to the speedy fall of Syracuse; but they were not 'home and dry' until reinforced by the ground troops, who were rapidly advancing inland. The whole operation—like that of the US 82nd Airborne, who went in on the same night—was a shambles, relieved only by acts of individual gallantry. There were many lessons to be learned from 'Fustian'; but since there was no time to absorb them before 1st Para Bde. was committed to Operation 'Marston' on 13 July, 'Marston', too, was a shambles.

The objective of Brig. Gerald Lathbury's brigade was the Primosole Bridge, an iron structure crossing the River Simeto some 25 miles along the coast from Augusta. The plan was for a small force of engineers and parachutists from the 1st Bn. to make a *coup de main* attack on the bridge itself by glider and parachute. The rest of the force (which now included 16th Parachute Field Ambulance, RAMC, and an Airborne Anti-Tank Troop, RA) would then land on DZs around the target and a glider LZ at the southern end of the bridge. For the first time a pathfinder force would be used to mark the DZs and LZ; this was the 21st Independent Parachute Company, AAC under Maj. John Lander, who would be setting up the 'Rebecca-Eureka' beacons for the first time ever on a parachute operation.

The fly-in was a disaster. The planned route took the USAAF pilots over landing beaches which, until only moments before, had been under heavy enemy air attack. The understandably nervous RN gunners crucified the low, slow Dakotas, and the entire force split up. Men were dropped as far away as Mt. Etna; others landed in the sea, and only some 295 men out of 2,000 actually made it to the bridge. Some stragglers from the 1st Para Bn. arrived with ominous news: they had been dropped some miles away on Catania airfield, and had found to their horror that they were using the same DZ as the German 4th Parachute Brigade, who had been dropped to reinforce the bridge.

Sure enough, the Fallschirmjäger attacked at dawn, and succeeded in surrounding the bridge. By 1800 hrs. on 14 July the 1st Para Bde. were forced to withdraw south and await 8th Army. When ground troops arrived the 9th Bn., The Durham Light Infantry put in a costly and ineffective attack against the German-held bridge. The next day they tried again, this time under the direction of Alistair Pearson of 1st Para Bn.; and after a stiff battle they drove the enemy off to the north.

Sicily fell on 17 August after a tough campaign; and almost immediately, the 1st Airborne Div. was ordered to prepare for an amphibious operation (!) in Italy. The 1st Air-Landing Bde. was in a terrible state after 'Fustian', and the 1st Parachute Bde. not much better off. These formations were kept in reserve, while the 2nd and 4th Para Bdes. sailed from Bizerta on 8 September. That night the Italians surrendered unconditionally; the landings at Taranto were unopposed, though 58 men from the 6th Para Bn. died when their ship, HMS *Abdiel*, struck a mine in the harbour.

Pushing inland rapidly, the 1st Airborne Div. captured first the town of Castellaneta, which was heavily defended by the Germans; and then, in a text-book assault by the untried 10th and 156th Para Bns., the town and airfield of Gioia. It was while watching the 10th Bn. in action here that the divisional commander, Maj. Gen. Hopkinson, was mortally wounded by an airburst shell. His place was taken by 'Dracula' Down, CO of the 2nd Para Bde.; the brigade was taken over by Lt. Col. C. V. H. Pritchard.

More hard fighting was expected to follow. In the event, however, the bulk of the division was withdrawn to the UK, arriving by sea in November 1943. Only the 2nd Para Bde. remained in Italy; expanded, and renamed '2nd Independent Parachute Bde. Gp.', they came under command of the 2nd New Zealand Infantry Division.

Back in England, the 4th Para Bde. were joined by the 11th Bn., who had been on detached service since the move to North Africa. They had carried out a company-strength operation on the Greek island of Kos, their DZ being marked by elements of the Special Boat Squadron. The drop went in on the night of 14 September 1943, and the Italian garrison surrendered in droves. Reinforcements from the Durham Light Infantry and the RAF Regiment soon arrived—as did the Luftwaffe, who bombed and strafed the force mercilessly in preparation for a seaborne counter-attack. Without

5 Para machine gun crew on top of the KKE Building in Constitution Square, Athens, December 1944. The .303in. Vickers Medium Machine Gun was the standard support company weapon of British infantry battalions throughout the war and into the late 1950s. Reliable and accurate in its sustained fire rôle, it was heavy and awkward to carry. For parachuting it was broken down into four loads (including extra ammo); like the PIAT and 3-in. mortar, it was carried by the strongest men in the battalion. The Hunting Stewart tartan patch behind the cap badge, inherited from 7th Bn., The Queen's Own Cameron Highlanders, from whom 5 Para were formed, is still worn today by 15 (Scottish) Para, one of the three current TA Para battalions. (Imp.War Museum)

air cover or further available reinforcements, the 11th Bn. detachment was withdrawn on 25 September. Another operation, planned against the island of Leros, was cancelled—to nobody's great dismay; and 11th Para Bn. arrived in England in December 1943.

The 2nd Ind. Para Bde. fought as infantry of the line throughout the long, wet Italian winter of 1943–44, taking steady casualties but receiving few replacements. A training unit and parachute school were eventually set up, first at Gioia and later, after the fall of Rome, at Lido di Roma. Volunteers from 8th Army units passed through these facilities before joining the brigade in the front line. A smaller parachute school set up near Monopoli on the Adriatic coast was used mainly by the special forces, SOE and commandos who inserted beach-marking and reconnaissance parties into occupied Yugoslavia prior to amphibious operations. One veteran of the Monopoli school remembers the weekend's course well. Only three jumps were required to qualify for parachute wings; but as these were made after only one day's instruction, without jumping helmets, and with ordinary bergen rucksacks and lengths of rope instead of proper kit bags, more than three jumps was reckoned to be pushing one's luck!

Loading a Horsa Mk. 1 glider; the wide door behind the cockpit was designed to take a jeep, and there were two smaller doors for personnel at the rear of the fuselage. These Royal Engineers (?) are loading the famous 'Airborne Bicycle', a folding machine used mainly by communications troops; some men jumped with them, others were dropped under their own 'chutes. (ABF Museum)

By March 1944, after a dismal spring spent patrolling not far north of the Tragino Aqueduct, the 2nd Bde. was a veteran unit. In that month they were sent to Cassino, where they remained until the end of May. On 1 June some 60 men of 6th Para Bn. carried out Operation 'Hasty', a diversionary attack on German demolition targets near Rimini. An entire German brigade was sent to flush them out; an entire division was held back from the main front to reinforce the rear areas; and the operation was generally a complete success, with only a few men captured.

Just over a month later came Operation 'Anvil', the invasion of southern France. Coming under the command of Maj. Gen. R. T. Frederick's 1st US Airborne Task Force, the brigade were given the job of capturing the area between the villages of La Motte and Le Muy some 15 miles inland from St. Tropez. D-Day was 15 August 1944; and by 0320 hrs. that day the pathfinders from 23rd Ind. Para Ptn. had set up the 'Rebecca-Eureka' beacons marking the DZ. Yet again, the drop was a shambles. Of 125 aircraft of the US 51st Troop Carrier Wing which set off from Rome, only 73

found the DZ. Some men landed as far away as Cannes, 20 miles down the coast. All the objectives were secured by mid-morning, however, and the LZs were cleared for the 61 incoming Horsa and Hadrian gliders carrying the 64th Lt. Bty., RA and the 300th Air-Landing Bty., RA. Their arrival was followed, on 17 August, by the leading elements of the ground forces. After some desultory patrolling, 2nd Ind. Para Bde. was withdrawn on 26 August.

Six weeks later they were in action again, this time in Greece. Under pressure from the Russian armies advancing westwards far to the north of their Balkan garrisons, the Germans had evacuated Athens by the beginning of October 1944; and, on the 12th, a reinforced company group from 4th Para Bn. landed in 30mph winds on Megara airfield some 40 miles west of the city. Casualties among the parachutists were understandably high: winds of 15 to 20mph are considered 'marginal conditions'. Despite losing half the force through injury, the paratroopers secured the airfield. The rest of the brigade followed two days later; but the race for Athens was lost on 15 October when the paratroopers entered the city hard on the heels of the 2nd Commando Brigade.

For the next three months the brigade fought its way from Athens to Salonika, near the Bulgarian frontier—but not just against the retreating Germans. The power-vacuum which they left in

Greece brought a number of heavily armed political factions on to the streets, and a full-scale civil war broke out. The brigade suffered heavy casualties. Nevertheless, the *ad hoc* British formation of which they were part ('Arkforce', which also included the 3rd and 23rd Armd. Bdes.) succeeded in beating the ELAS guerillas; in feeding some 20,000 starving Greeks each day, for an extended period; and—to some, the most gratifying success of all—in winning outspoken support from a previously hostile British trade union delegation who were investigating unfounded rumours of brutality by the airborne troops.

In January 1945 the brigade was withdrawn to Italy for further operations. Between 6 March and 4 May 1945 no less than 32 operations were planned, but none took place. With the end of the war, 2nd Independent Parachute Brigade returned to the UK in June 1945 to join the 6th Airborne Division.

North-West Europe 1943–45

Prelude to Invasion

There were now two complete Airborne Divisions in the British order of battle: the 1st, recently returned from North Africa and Italy, and the 6th, newly formed under Richard Gale. There had been some changes in their respective line-ups since Christmas 1943, but the divisional structure was settled as shown in Tables 1 and 2.

Among the Air-Landing troops there had been a complete reshuffle. The 6th Air-Landing Bde. had been formed from the 2nd Bn., The Oxfordshire and Buckinghamshire Light Infantry; the 1st Bn., The Royal Ulster Rifles (both these two units being transferred from 1st Air-Landing Bde.); and the 12th Bn., The Devonshire Regiment. The 1st Air-Landing Bde. now consisted of the 2nd Bn., The South Staffordshire Regiment; the 1st Bn., The Border Regiment; and the 7th Bn., The King's Own Scottish Borderers.

The 3rd Parachute Bde. consisted of the 1st Canadian Para Bn. under Lt. Col. G. F. P. Bradbrooke; the 8th Para Bn. under Lt. Col. Alistair Pearson (who had been sent home after contracting malaria in Italy); and the 9th Para Bn.

Interior of a Horsa glider, looking forward. In the original print a Bren and a PIAT can be seen at the front; the rest of these Air-Landing soldiers carry the ubiquitous Lee-Enfield No. 4. Beneath the men's legs on the floor lie A-frame bergen rucksacks. Apart from the metal floor, the entire structure was wood: the chances of escaping a crash-landing unhurt were extremely slim. (ABF Museum)

Table 1: 1st Airborne Division, 1941–45

Div. HQ
1 A'bne. Div. Sigs. Sqn; 21 Indep. Para Coy, AAC (Pathfinders); 1 Air-Lndg. Recce Sqn; A'bne. Lt. Tank Sqn, RAC

Div. Troops
RE: 9 Fd. Coy; 261 Fd.Park Coy; 1, 2, 3 & 4 Para Sqns; 1, 9 & 591 A'bne.Sqns; 261 A'bne. Park Sqn
RA: 1 Air-Lndg.Lt.Bty; 1 Air-Lndg.Lt.Regt; 204 Indep., 1, 2 & 5 Air-Lndg.A/T Bties; 1 Air-Lndg.A/T Regt; 1 & 283 Lt.A/A Bties

1st Parachute Brigade
1, 2 & 3 Para Bns; 4 Para Bn (until July '42); B Coy, 13 Para Bn (att. May '45); 17 Para Bn. *Under command* 16 Para Fd.Amb., RAMC. (Infantry and armoured detachments also served under 1 Para Bde. in Norway.)

4th Parachute Brigade
10, 11 & 156 Para Bns. *Under command* 133 Fd.Amb. RAMC

1st Air-Landing Brigade
1 Border Regt, 2 South Staffordshire Regt, 7 King's Own Scottish Borderers, *2 Ox. & Bucks.Lt.Inf., *1 Royal Ulster Rifles (*both bns. transferred to 6th Air-Lndg.Bde., May '43.) *Under command* 458 Lt.Bty & 223 A/T Bty, RA; 1 Air-Lndg.Bde.Gp.Coy, RASC; 181 Fd.Amb., RAMC; 1 Air-Lndg.Bde.Gp.Provo Section, RMP.

Table 2: 6th Airborne Division, 1943–48

Div. HQ
6 A'bne. Div. Sigs. Sqn; 22 Indep. Para Coy, AAC (Pathfinders); 6 A'bne.Div.Armd.Recce Regt, RAC; 1 A'bne.Lt.Tank Sqn, RAC
Div. Troops
RE: 249 A'bne.Fd.Coy; 3 & 591 Para Sqns; 3 & 9 A'bne.Sqns; 286 A'bne.Fd.Park Coy
RA: 3 & 4 Air-Lndg. A/T Bties; 53 (Worcs.Yeo) & 2 Air-Lndg.A/T Regts; 2 Air-Lndg.Lt.A/A Bty
3rd Parachute Brigade
8 (Midlands Counties), 9 (Home Counties), & 1 (Canadian) Para Bns; 7 (Lt.Inf.) Para Bn (until August '43); 3 Para Bn (from August '45)
5th Parachute Brigade
12 & 13 Para Bns; 7 (Lt.Inf.) Para Bn (from August '43)
Under command in Far East 4 Air-Lndg.A/T Bty, RA; 3 A'bne.Sqn, RE; 22 Indep.Para Coy, AAC; Para Ptn., 716 Lt.Composite Coy, RASC; 225 Para Fd.Amb., RAMC
6th Air-Landing Brigade
2 Ox. & Bucks.Lt.Inf., 12 Devonshire Regt, 1 Royal Ulster Rifles. (Bde. detached from Div., November '45, to become 23 Infantry Brigade)

under Lt. Col. T. B. H. Otway. The formation was commanded by Brig. James Hill. Their sister brigade, the 5th, under Brig. J. H. N. Poett, consisted of the 7th (Light Infantry) Para Bn., the 12th (Yorkshire) Para Bn., and the 13th (Lancashire) Para Battalion.

The 1st Airborne Division was unchanged. Maj. Gen. Down was subsequently posted to India to take over the 44th Indian Airborne Div., and command fell upon Maj. Gen. Roy Urquhart, a shy, dour Scotsman.

Airborne Forces had been regularised. As mentioned above, The Parachute Regiment had been formed on 1 August 1942. All ranks wore the maroon beret with, from that date, the cap badge of the Army Air Corps; but in May 1943 a cap badge was created for The Parachute Regiment. This was a parachute supported by two wings with, above it, the royal lion and king's crown (the 'dog and basket'). Headquarters Airborne Forces was established at Syrancote House, near Netheravon; and 'Boy' Browning, who had been created 'Major-General Airborne Forces' in June 1943, was now promoted lieutenant-general, and established himself there with his staff.

On the air side, too, things had changed. On 15 January 1942 HQ 38 Wing RAF was formed, with responsibility for the training of parachutists and glider pilots. No. 1 Parachute Training School already existed, as did No. 1 Glider Training School. A second glider school was set up, as were operational training units and parachute and glider exercise squadrons. On 11 October 1943 the Wing became a Group, under Air Vice-Marshal L. N. Hollinghurst; on 22 November 1943 it was placed under command of HQ Allied Expeditionary Forces. The Group was to supply the gliders and tugs for the invasion, as well as flying in the pathfinders. No. 46 Group RAF was formed in February 1944, and equipped with Dakotas; they would fly in as many British paratroops as possible, the USAAF carrying the rest. Both groups carried out extensive combat operations during the early part of 1944, varying their operational diet by resupplying—and occasionally inserting—resistance, sabotage and SAS groups into the occupied nations of Europe.

Richard Gale was meanwhile putting together a plan for the airborne phase of the invasion. He had been given a number of vital jobs on the left flank of the beachhead; and with just one division, he had somehow to achieve complete success in order to give the main amphibious forces the best possible chance. The main tasks were: to destroy several bridges vital to the enemy's reinforcements; to capture and hold two bridges over the River Orne and the Caen Canal which were vital to our own forces; to destroy the gun battery at Merville which overlooked the landing beaches; and to occupy a blocking position near the Bois de Bavent in order to hold off enemy reinforcements.

The planning of and preparation for these operations were critically important. The 5th Para Bde. was to take the Orne and Caen Canal bridges, then to secure LZs for the main glider lift on the evening of D-Day. The 3rd Para Bde. was to destroy the Merville battery; to destroy as many bridges as they could in the Varaville, Robehomme, Bures and Troarn area; and then to form a defensive perimeter to the south-east around the Bois de Bavent. The 6th Air-Landing Bde. would arrive in the second lift, less the 12th Devons, who would arrive by sea—a decision forced by the perennial shortage of aircraft and gliders.

Maj. Gen. Gale (inevitably known to all—but not to his face—as 'Windy') concluded his final briefing with these words: 'What you get by stealth and guts, you must hold by skill and determination.' Brig. James Hill told his 3rd Para Bde.: 'Gentlemen, in spite of your excellent training and orders, do not be daunted if chaos reigns. It undoubtedly will.'

D-Day, 6 June 1944

The first Allied troops to leave for the invasion were the pathfinders of 6th Airborne Div., 22nd Independent Parachute Company, AAC. They took off from Harwell near Oxford at 2303 hrs. on 5 June; like the party taking the two bridges, they were due over the target at 0020 hrs. on the 6th, and there they duly appeared.

The *coup de main* party tasked with the capture of the bridges consisted of D Coy., 2nd 'Ox and Bucks', commanded by Maj. R. J. Howard, with a sapper detachment. Their six Horsas deposited them right on top of the target: three landed within 50 yards of the canal bridge. Howard led a brisk attack against the objective, securing it within 15

minutes for the cost of one man killed. A counter-attack led by three elderly tanks was beaten off with a PIAT some minutes later.

A few hundred yards to the east Lt. D. B. Fox led the attack on the Orne bridge, which was initially unopposed. Counter-attacks soon made both bridges unhealthy spots, however; and despite reinforcement by the 7th Para Bn. at a later stage, the defence of the bridges became a trial of endurance. The Germans even sent gunboats against the airborne soldiers; but to no avail. Even further to the east, the pathfinders had found themselves in serious trouble. High winds had scattered the aircraft, and it was virtually impossible to mark the DZs and LZs in the 30 minutes allotted for the task: virtually, but not completely, and the zones were marked. Even so, the 3rd and 5th Para Bdes. were scattered like chaff.

Normandy, 6 June 1944: DZs and LZs marked here are mainly notional—the drops were widely scattered, and only the *coup de main* **party at 'Pegasus Bridge' went in as planned.**

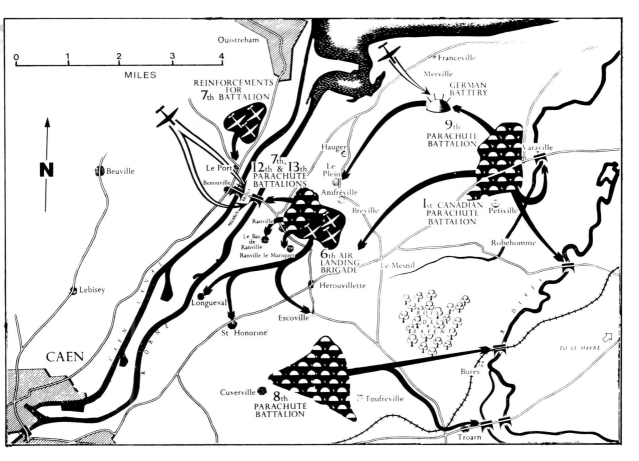

The eve of D-Day: Pathfinders chat with their aircrews before emplaning. These crews were all from No. 38 Group, RAF Army Co-operation Command, and were considered among the bravest and most skilled in the service. The officer from 22 Indep.Coy., at right, wears the Army Air Corps cap-badge on his maroon beret; he seems to be wearing a life jacket beneath his 'chute harness. The man on the left carries a Eureka radio beacon, used to guide Rebecca-equipped aircraft to the DZ. Both men wear the 1943 sleeveless Jacket, Parachutist over their Denison smocks. (ABF Museum)

The first soldier from the 7th Bn. to touch the ground was the deputy adjutant, a young actor in peacetime, whose name was Richard Todd. His battalion's task was to relieve the *coup de main* party at the bridges as soon as possible; this they did, though by first light less than 200 of the widely scattered paratroopers had assembled. (By coincidence, some 20 years later, Richard Todd was to star in the film '*The Longest Day*'—playing Maj. John Howard in the attack on the bridges!)

The 12th Para Bn. had captured the village of Le Bas de Ranville by 1100 hrs. on D-Day, and remained there for some time, fighting off repeated and ever-heavier German counter-attacks. Joined by the 13th Bn., they held out until relieved by the Commandos of Brig. The Lord Lovat's 1st Special Service Brigade.

The 9th Para Bn. had been given the toughest job of all, and were to suffer most from the adverse weather. The Merville battery had to be taken at all costs, so the resourceful Terence Otway rehearsed his battalion in a specially landscaped field near Newbury. Nine separate rehearsals and five days of minutely detailed briefing preceded the drop; all 635 officers and men could have found their way around the battery blindfold. It was decided that the main force of paratroopers and sappers should storm the target from ground level, while three glider-loads of volunteers would land right on top of the battery just ten minutes after a saturation bombing raid by RAF Lancasters. The best-laid plans . . .

The situation after the drop is best described in Otway's terse report: 'By 0250 hrs. the Battalion had grown to 150 strong, with 20 lengths of Bangalore torpedo. Each company was approximately 30 strong. Enough Signals to carry on; no 3in. mortars; one machine gun; one half of one sniping party; no 6pdr. guns; no jeeps or trailers, or any glider stores; no sappers; no field ambulance, but six unit medical orderlies; no mine detectors; one company commander missing. The commanding officer decided to advance immediately.'

Otway, as might be expected, was in a foul temper. Nevertheless, the battalion was organised and in the right place at the right time for the glider force to go in. None of the gliders actually made it to the battery; one, piloted by Staff Sgt. D. F. Kerr, survived a landing in a minefield and a four-hour fire-fight with German reinforcements rushing to the nearby battery.

Shouting 'Everybody in! We're going to take this bloody battery!', Otway urged his battalion into the objective. When he led them out again there were only 80 left—but the guns had been destroyed. The survivors immediately moved off to their secondary objective, the high ground above the village of Le Plein. There they kept 200 Germans bottled up in a château until relieved by the Commandos.

Scattered to the four winds, the 8th Para Bn. had fared little better. Pearson never faltered, however: his orders were to blow the Bures and Troarn bridges, and despite being wounded on the DZ he set out to do this, dividing his 180 men (of some 600 who had dropped) into two parties. They succeeded in blowing two of the three allocated bridges, but had not got enough explosive left for the third until their 'attached' sappers finally managed to join up with them. After a gung-ho jeep ride through the village of Troarn—and its German roadblock— they reached the bridge, and destroyed it. That evening, established in the Bois de Bavent, Pearson instituted an aggressive programme of fighting patrols which convinced the Germans that his one undersized battalion was something the size of a brigade.

The 1st Canadian Para Bn. managed to destroy the Varaville and Robehomme bridges despite being spread over an area ten times the size of their assigned DZ; following their original plan, they withdrew to Le Mesnil, where they linked up with the rest of the division.

The battle of Breville

As in Sicily, the widely dispersed drop put the fear of God into many German soliders. Convinced that more than three divisions had dropped, the enemy were initially confused as to where the actual invasion was, and whether all this activity might not be a diversion for the real invasion elsewhere. They learned soon enough, however: the Wehrmacht was not slow on the uptake, and their powers

The dawn of D-Day: glider troops from D Coy., 2nd Bn., Oxfordshire and Buckinghamshire Light Infantry, who took the Orne River and Caen Canal bridges shortly after midnight on 5/6 June 1944. Note the toggle ropes worn as belts— practical, and comfortable. The officer in the centre carries a Mk. V Sten SMG, with pistol-grip forestock and 'pig-sticker' bayonet. Both the other men seem to carry revolvers in addition to their primary weapons. (Imp.War Museum)

of organisation and quick response were legendary. Before long a number of heavy counter-attacks developed, and it became necessary for the division to concentrate and present a united front.

By dawn on D + 1 the division was in more or less the right place, in more or less good shape, and the Air-Landing elements had arrived more or less on time. As Lovat's Commandos had now come under Gale's command, he had a strong force with fairly secure lines of communication back to the beachhead.

From D + 2 (8 June) onwards, however, there was no respite. The Germans had to break through at the village of Breville in order to attack the beaches. This route lay between the 3rd Para Bde. and the 1st Special Service Bde., and the village itself remained in German hands throughout the week following the invasion. Repeated attacks had so weakened Gale's division that he took a calculated risk when he threw his final reserve into one final effort to take Breville. On the night of 12 June the 12th Para Bn., a company of the 12th Devons, the pathfinder company and a squadron of tanks went in, all of them much under strength. In the battle which followed 12 Para lost their CO, Lt. Col. A. P. Johnson, and 140 other men; the Devons lost 36 men dead and wounded; but Breville fell, and remained in British hands, finally securing the

Ranville LZ, Normandy, after the second D-Day lift had landed: this shows just how many gliders crowded on to the LZ. The tail section of the Horsa could be removed to allow large loads out quickly; in some cases the large bolts which secured it got jammed, and jeeps and hawsers were used to break the fuselage instead. Some of the anti-glider stakes—'Rommelspargeln'—erected by the Germans are still in evidence here; most were removed by Pathfinders and Engineers jumping with the first lift. (Imp.War Museum)

left flank of the invasion.

For the next two months the situation remained fairly static. Aggressive patrolling was the order of the day. There was no question of pulling the 6th Airborne Div. out of the battle: they were too valuable where they were, so, like their comrades of the 1st Para Bde. in Tunisia, they fought on as infantry of the line.

Finally, on 17 August, orders were given for a break-out. The 6th Airborne were to work their way along the coast towards the River Seine, and there secure what crossings they could. With commandeered transport and a great deal of imaginative planning, Gale kept the retreating enemy under such pressure that he reached the Seine on 26 August. Only then, after three months' continuous action, was the division withdrawn and placed in reserve.

The Stillborne Division

While the 6th Airborne had been fighting in Normandy, great things were happening elsewhere. A combined formation composed of the two British airborne divisions and three American (the 17th, 82nd and 101st) was created, designated 1st Allied

Airborne Army, under the command of a USAAF general, Lt. Gen. Lewis Brereton. (By coincidence, Brereton had been on the planning staff of the US 1st Div. in France in 1918 when it had been proposed that the formation be dropped behind the Kaiser's lines by parachute. A subaltern serving with the same division now commanded the three divisions of the 18th US Airborne Corps—Lt. Gen. Matthew B. Ridgway.)

More important for the British, there now existed a similar formation in their own order of battle: 1st Airborne Corps, commanded by Browning, had been formed in 1943 and consisted of the two British divisions and the recently-formed 1st Polish Independent Parachute Brigade, led by the tough, experienced Maj. Gen. Stanislaw Sosabowski.

The only people who were not happy with life were the 1st Airborne Division. After spending the early part of 1944 making good their losses from the Mediterranean campaigns and training with 6th Airborne, the division was in splendid form and aching for action. They were disappointed at being held in reserve during the invasion, and more disappointed when they were not used at all. Disappointment turned first to boredom, and then to cynicism; believing—as many then did—that the war would be over before they got another chance to fight, the men called themselves the '1st Stillborne Division'. In fact as many as 16 operations were planned, only to be abandoned as the rapid advance of the ground forces made them pointless—on one occasion, when the men were actually preparing to emplane. The one operation which might have got off the ground was 'Comet', an assault on the waterways between Belgium and the Ruhr which was planned for 7 September 1944. It was considered to have an excellent chance of success, as the German defenders were in total disarray at the time; but bad weather forced its postponement, and by 10 September the opportunity had passed. The idea had been good, however; and it was to be resurrected by no less a figure than the commander of 21st Army Group, Field Marshal Montgomery.

In spite of strong criticism from his American rival, Patton, Monty persuaded Eisenhower to let him try a full-blooded thrust towards the Ruhr. Eisenhower had been under a certain amount of light pressure from Washington to get the 1st Allied Airborne Army into action; he was reluctantly impressed by Monty's plan, and gave it the go-ahead.

The news that another operation was in the offing was greeted by the 1st Airborne Div. with a certain amount of scepticism, but they set to, not expecting much to come of the idea. In a few cases boredom had got the better of the men. A severe attack of it in 1st Para Bn. was punished by the 1st Para Bde. commander, Brig. Lathbury, in true Airborne style: on this operation the 2nd and 3rd Bns. would jump first.

Arnhem

Operation 'Market Garden' was Montgomery's attempt to end the war by Christmas 1944. That it ended in failure cannot be blamed either on Montgomery, or on the airborne soldiers who fought so bravely in the spearhead. Monty's plan was simple, and uncharacteristically audacious: the British 2nd Army, under Gen. Miles Dempsey, would make a 60-mile dash from Neerpelt on the Belgian/Dutch border to Arnhem on the Rhine, so outflanking the German 'West Wall' by the north. Three airborne divisions would drop to capture vital crossings over the many rivers and canals which barred Dempsey's path, and would hold them until relieved by the advancing armour. The US 101st Airborne would capture the bridges over the Wilhelmina and Willems canals at Son and Veghel respectively; the US 82nd Airborne would take the Maas and Waal bridges at Grave and Nijmegen; and the British 1st Airborne, penetrating furthest behind enemy lines, would capture the road and rail bridges across the Rhine at Arnhem. For this operation the three divisions were placed under the command of 'Boy' Browning, now Brereton's deputy at 1st Allied Airborne Army.

At Montgomery's planning conference in Brussels on 10 September Lt. Gen. Browning received his orders. He was told that XXX Corps, the 2nd Army spearhead commanded by Lt. Gen. Brian Horrocks, would reach Arnhem in 48 hours. Browning reckoned that 1st Airborne could hold out for four days if necessary; but added the now-immortal qualification, 'But, sir, I think we may be going a bridge too far.' (The rewriting of history which put these words in his mouth *after* the battle in a recent, fictionalised feature film is felt by some who knew him to be one of a number of regrettable libels on Browning's character and intelligence.)

For their part the 1st Airborne were delighted to be going into action. The fact that they had only one week to plan and mount the operation did not alarm them unduly.

For Roy Urquhart the first problem was logistics: there were not enough aircraft to get the whole division to Arnhem in one lift. He elected to take 1st Para Bde. and 1st Air-Landing Bde. with Div. HQ on D-Day, the former to seize the bridge by *coup de main*, the latter to guard the DZs and LZs for the later lifts. The second lift, on D + 1, would consist of the 4th Para Bde.; the third, on D + 2, would consist of the 1st Polish Ind. Para Bde. The plan was for 1st Para Bde. to hold the bridges for 24 hours; 4th Para Bde. would then take the high ground north of Arnhem, while 1st Air-Landing Bde. would create a perimeter to the west in the suburb of Oosterbeek. The Poles would land south of the river, then cross it to create a perimeter to the east.

Two studies in officerlike dress: Maj.Gen. Richard 'Windy' Gale, GOC 6th Airborne Div. (left), wearing a type of Denison smock for officers, with pale fawn knit cuffs and collar lining, and a full-length zip. He wears it over his BD blouse, and officer's field breeches. The lieutenant (right) wears skeleton-order '37 webbing over a combat uniform indistinguishable from any other Airborne soldier; he carries a Mk. V Sten with a wooden butt, and a holstered revolver. The picture was taken at 6th Airborne's Div. HQ shortly after D-Day. (Imp.War Museum)

Rare aerial reconnaissance photo of the Arnhem road bridge, taken on 6 September 1944. Note the open ground to the south of the river (right); and the built-up area to the north (left), in which 2 Para made their heroic stand two weeks later. The bridge was destroyed by the Germans shortly before they withdrew from Holland in 1945. (ABF Museum)

That, as they say, was the plan . . .

Urquhart's other headache was the choice of DZs available. The open ground south of the river was 'unsuitable', according to the RAF; besides, flak over Arnhem, and the Luftwaffe airfield to the north at Deelen, made heavy losses among the aircraft almost inevitable. The RAF therefore suggested the open ground west of Oosterbeek, some seven miles from the bridge. Urquhart reluctantly agreed, but only because enemy strength in Arnhem was believed to be low. Despite disquieting rumours from the Dutch Resistance, HQ 1st Allied Airborne Army received no hard information suggesting otherwise.

The drop was planned for noon on 17 September. First to arrive, on DZ 'X', were Maj. B. A. Wilson's divisional pathfinders of 21st Ind. Para Coy.; they were followed by Div. HQ, 1st Air-Landing Bde., and 1st Para Bde. in that order. Despite aircraft losses en route the drop was virtually faultless, and the troops quickly set off on their alloted tasks.

First away were 'Freddie Gough's Specials': the 1st Air-Landing Recce Squadron. Moving in armoured jeeps, they were to take the bridges by surprise attack. The 2nd Para Bn., led by Frost, were to make for the bridges on foot, taking a route which followed the river and by-passed Oosterbeek.

Further north, 3rd Para Bn. would move through Oosterbeek in the same direction; and 1st Para Bn. were in reserve.

Taking a more northerly route than either 2 or 3 Para, Gough's men were soon encountering stiff resistance. While Gough himself returned to Div. HQ to report to Urquhart, Frost and Fitch pressed on alone, unaware that the 'Specials' had not reached the bridges. Urquhart did not even know where the 'Specials' were: he had been told that none of their jeeps had arrived. Worse still, none of the radio sets seemed to be working. He decided to go forward and warn Lathbury in person that 2 Para were on their own.

At 1630 hrs. that afternoon the operation began to go seriously wrong. An SS training batallion under Maj. Sepp Krafft, who had actually seen the drop, took up a blocking position between the DZ and the bridges. Here, just east of Wolfhezen, he fought off both 3 Para and 1 Para. He did not yet know it, but he was aided in this by no less a formation than Gen. Wilhelm Bittrich's 2nd SS Panzer Corps, consisting of the 9th 'Hohenstaufen' and 10th 'Frundsberg' SS Panzer Divisions. Receiving news of the airborne attack, Bittrich ordered his two divisions, led by Lt. Col. Walter Harzer and Brig. Heinz Harmel respectively, out of Arnhem to repulse this advance. Their presence here was totally unexpected: as already stated, no firm intelligence had reached Browning suggesting that they were in the area in any sort of strength. But here they were, even if in depleted numbers after hard fighting in France; and they were as determined to fight as these crack units always were. A recce batallion under Capt. Paul Gräbner was sent to check the bridges; finding nobody there, Gräbner was ordered to Nijmegen. While he patrolled slowly down the Arnhem–Nijmegen highway, Frost's 2 Para arrived at the road bridge.

Hampered, like everyone else, by the communications breakdown, Frost ordered A Coy.—by then his only available sub-unit—to rush the northern end of the bridge. After a stiff fight they were successful, and were joined by Gough and his men. A second attack, this time to capture the southern end, was unsuccessful: Gräbner had left some of his SS Panzergrenadiers there as a garrison. Lt. John Grayburn tried to lead his men across the bridge twice, but was beaten back both times, while a fierce battle raged around the northern end.

The rest of the brigade were fighting an increasingly desperate battle with the German defenders. Urquhart and Lathbury were cut off from the rest of the division; but by dawn on the 18th, D + 1, they were up with 3rd Para Bn., urging them on. Concerned about the rest of the division—there had been no news for several hours—the two officers decided to make their way back to Div. HQ, now established at the Hartenstein Hotel in Oosterbeek. While they were moving back Lathbury was seriously wounded. Urquhart helped carry him to shelter; then shot a German soldier with his Colt .45 automatic when the man appeared at the window of the house in which they were taking cover—one of the few modern occasions when a divisional commander has got close enough to see the whites of the enemy's eyes. Moving through the town, Urquhart's small party got trapped yet again, and the general had to shelter for the rest of the day and the night which followed in the attic of a house.

Back at the DZs, Hick's Air-Landing Bde. had also had a rough night fending off repeated attacks.

When the 4th Para Bde. dropped that day, four hours late due to fog over the British airfields, they found the DZs clear but a stiff battle in progress. 'Shan' Hackett himself accepted the surrender of several Germans on the DZ before he could even assemble his HQ. The news of Urquhart's absence, and the shambles to which the operation had degenerated, shocked the brigade commander.

Urquhart had named Hicks as his successor after Lathbury, and Hicks now ordered Hackett to send his 11th Para Bn. towards the bridges to support the by now badly mauled 1st Para Bde.; in exchange, Hackett should have 7 KOSB from the Air-Landing Bde.; and the 2nd South Staffords, now released from DZ garrison duties, could lead 11th Para into Arnhem.

During the rest of the 18th, the night which followed, and the morning of the 19th, 4th Para

17 September 1944: men of the 1st Parachute Bde. draw and fit their 'chutes for Operation 'Market Garden'. The sleeveless Jacket, Parachutist is much in evidence. The centre man wears his webbing under it and his small pack reversed on his chest. He is adjusting the shoulder buckles of his mate's X-Type harness so that when the canopy opens he will hang below it at the correct angle. (ABF Museum)

Arnhem: the approach. The seven-mile march from the DZs and LZs to Arnhem bridge was carried out at walking pace through heavily wooded countryside and tree-lined lanes—ideal ambush country. Here a jeep is towing a 6-pdr. anti-tank gun landed from one of the gliders. (ABF Museum)

Arnhem, and the DZs and LZs of 1st Airborne Div.: it is easy, with hindsight, to see how much better off the division would have been if they had been dropped to the south and east of the two road bridges (immediately north of DZ 'K' on this map).

Bde. tried to carry out their alloted task, but they were repeatedly beaten back with heavy casualties. The Polish glider LZ at Wolfhezen was being guarded by 7 KOSB at this time, in anticipation of the third lift. The Polish glider element duly arrived—but not their paratroopers, who were held up on fog-bound UK airfields. The Poles who did arrive took heavy casualties on the LZ, but somehow managed to retain some semblance of order, and fought bravely and well with the rest of the division. Later on the 19th the 4th Para Bde. were ordered to withdraw to a divisional perimeter which had been established around Oosterbeek.

The withdrawal from contact was an epic in itself. All three of Hackett's battalions had taken a beating. Hackett personally led his HQ and other elements in a series of bayonet charges through the thick woods south-east of Wolfhezen. Battered, and disgusted at the turn of events, the brigade took up positions on the north-east corner of the perimeter: 7 KOSB nearest the railway line, 156 Para next to them, and 10 Para on the now-notorious Ooster-

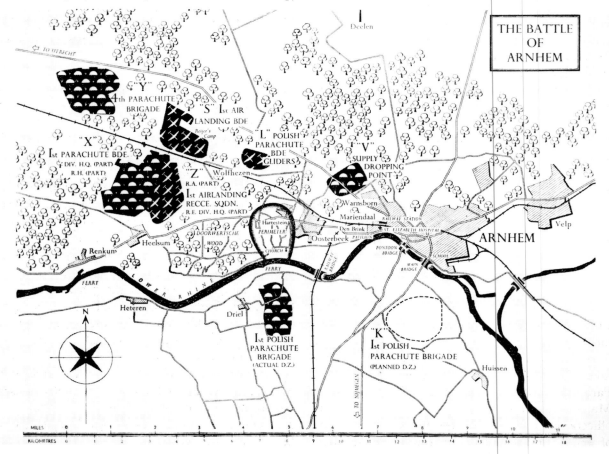

THE BATTLE OF ARNHEM

beek crossroads. To the right of 10 Para was a composite battalion—'Lonsdale Force', after its CO, Maj. Dickie Lonsdale, second in command of 11 Para—comprising elements of 1st, 2nd and 3rd Para Bns., 11th Para Bn., and the South Staffords. The Border Regiment, the pathfinders of 21st Independent Co., and the glider pilots held the western perimeter along with Royal Engineers.

To everyone's relief, Urquhart had managed to rejoin early on the morning of the 19th, D + 2. He organised the withdrawal and the defence of the perimeter; and had had to face the agonising decision to abandon 2nd Para Bn. to its fate, since there was now no hope of linking up with the bridge. Despite the communications problems he was able to make occasional contact with Browning at Nijmegen, via the division's rear link in the UK; and he urged that the Poles be dropped near the village of Driel, some six miles west of their planned DZ. He hoped that they would be able to cross the river from there, and link up with the exhausted division.

It was not to be. The Poles arrived two days late, on 21 September, and every attempt to get more than a few men across was beaten back by the Germans. In the end Sosabowski had to dig in on the south bank and wait for XXX Corps to arrive.

Meanwhile, resistance at the bridge had finally ceased. Frost was wounded on the morning of 20 September, D + 3, and Freddie Gough took over command at the bridge. For another 24 hours the 'Red Devils' of 2 Para clung to its northern end with desperate ferocity. A short truce late on 20 September allowed the wounded to be taken into German captivity; then the fighting began again. One by one the men ran out of ammunition, and by shortly after first light on 21 September the position had been overrun. Out of some 700 men who had first fortified the houses overlooking the Rhine, barely 100 now remained.

Things were no better back at the division. Constant shelling and mortaring, and attacks by infantry with tanks and SP guns, had taken a terrible toll of the defenders. The 4th Para Bde. had taken the worst casualties: by 22 September, 156th Para Bn. was down to 100 men under command of Maj. Geoffrey Powell; 10th Para Bn. had lost all its officers, and all but 30 men—of these, the survivors of some 500 who had jumped, only 16 men were

Arnhem, during the early days: a 1st Airborne Div. intelligence officer interrogates a German Army senior NCO captured during the advance into the town. The presence of II SS Panzer Korps was never suspected by the division. (Imp. War Museum)

destined to escape from the closing trap.

Only one hope kept the men going—the presence across the river of XXX Corps. Fighting slowly forward along a single, narrow axis of advance which was defended grimly by the SS Panzers of Harmel's division, the leading elements of the Guards Armoured Division had crossed the Waal at Nijmegen on the afternoon of the 20th. The bridge had been captured for them by one of the bravest assault river crossings of the war, mounted by the 3rd Bn., 504th Parachute Infantry Regt. of the US 82nd Airborne Division. The tank advance was soon halted, however, and the 5th Bn., Duke of Cornwall's Light Infantry had to be brought forward to 'take point' for the 43rd Infantry Division. They eventually linked up with Sosabowski on the south bank of the Rhine late on 22 September. That night the abortive attempt to ferry the Poles across the river was shot to pieces, only some 50 men making it to the far bank. The next attempt was made by the 4th Dorsets; barely half of them succeeded.

Second lift to Arnhem: 4th Parachute Bde. arrive, to be met with strong resistance. The sky is very crowded indeed—2,000 parachutists, all jumping more or less at once, tend to get in each other's way; careful training of parachutists is essential if there are not to be fatal mistakes in circumstances like these. (Imp.War Museum)

Urquhart had by this time managed to get his chief of staff, Col. Charles Mackenzie, across the river to liaise with XXX Corps. Browning was also in the area, and he agreed with Maj. Gen. Thomas, commanding the 43rd Div., that the 1st Airborne should be evacuated from their shrinking perimeter. Crossing back over the Rhine, Mackenzie passed this message to Urquhart on the morning of 25 September. Urquhart's heart must have sunk at the prospect: the only way out was across the Rhine, the way the Poles had tried to get in.

That night Operation 'Berlin', the extraction of the Airborne survivors, took place. Urquhart designed the operation to give the impression to the enemy that a fierce fight was still going on. With the wounded and certain selected units holding out to the last, the division moved silently to the crossing point. Most of the men were furious to think that after fighting for so long and at such cost, it was all to be for nothing. The evacuation lasted all night, and by first light on 26 September all were across who were going across: just 2,163 men, out of the 10,005 who had begun to land around Arnhem nine days before.

At least 1,500 Airborne soldiers were killed during the battle. They lie today in Oosterbeek cemetery where, every year on the anniversary, Dutch children lay flowers on their graves. A guard of honour from 10 Para—the only British parachute battalion to have survived since 1944 without being renumbered or amalgamated—mount guard over the graves of the men who helped create the legend of the Red Beret. Their epitaph may be taken from the words of the official account of the battle:

'In attack most daring, in defence most cunning, in endurance most steadfast, they performed a feat of arms which will be remembered and recounted as long as the virtues of courage and resolution have power to move the hearts of men.

'Now these things befell at Arnhem.'

The Aftermath

Despite Montgomery's assertion that 'Market Garden' was 90% successful, the loss of almost the entire 1st Airborne Div. raised some awkward questions. Too many factors contributed to the disaster for the blame to be laid at any one door; but one of Brig. Jim Gavin's comments before the operation bears close attention—that it was 'better to suffer 10% initial casualties by dropping either on or close to the bridge, than to run the risk of landing on distant drop zones.'

Airborne forces are too lightly armed to rely on anything but surprise and concentration for the success of their operations. Given that only two brigades could be landed on D-Day, these factors assumed vital significance. It is a fallacy that the British had fewer aircraft than either of the two American divisions: in fact, they had slightly more. But the decision to fly Browning's Corps HQ to Nijmegen absorbed a battalion's lift of gliders, while the jeeps and trailers which landed at Wolfhezen on D-Day could have been sacrificed to allow more men into the battle.

Once the element of surprise was lost on D-Day, and the already small force was split up between the DZs and the bridge, the 4th Para Bde.'s arrival was bound to be an 'event'. In a letter to the present writer Gen. Hackett wrote:

'The choice of DZs (especially for my own brigade, when surprise had been lost and we came in on the second wave) was disastrous. As I understood it at the time the choice of dropping zone so far away from the objective was forced upon the operation by exaggerated fears of the extent of German anti-aircraft defences in the neighbourhood of Deelen Airfield. I have not closely studied all the documents, but my impression is that the RAF were strongly opposed to what they regarded as an invitation to heavy casualties if they took us in any closer, whereas we were prepared to risk these to be dropped close enough to our objectives.

'It may interest you to know that in my own final conference before take-off I went through the plan for my brigade's occupation of a defensive position around the north side of Arnhem city with meticulous care and all the briefing material (which in terms of terrain was very good indeed) available. I then dismissed all the officers of the brigade who were present except the battalion commanders and the brigade staff, and told them that they could forget all that. Being put down where we were, with surprise gone and the opposition alerted, and given the German capability for a swift and violent response to any threat to what really mattered, they could expect their hardest fighting and worst casualties, not in defence of the final perimeter, but in trying to get there. And of course, we never did, though nobody, I am quite sure, could have tried harder.'

Gen. Hackett had the highest regard for the RAF but not, perhaps, for their tactical appreciation of ground matters. It was fitting, however, that of the

Arnhem: a British paratrooper caught by the camera of an unknown Dutch civilian. He carries a Mk. V Sten, and a pistol hangs on his right thigh in a low-slung Royal Armoured Corps holster with a thigh strap. Webbing is limited to light belt order. Note how the chamois-lined 'bellows' pocket on the left thigh of the 'Airborne' BD trousers is distended by a load of ammunition and grenades. (ABF Museum)

6-pdr. A/T gun in action near Oosterbeek; this weapon has the battle-honour GALLIPOLI painted on the inside of the gunshield. It was while using one of these guns to fend off German SPGs that L/Sgt. John Baskeyfield of the 2nd South Staffords won his posthumous Victoria Cross. (ABF Museum)

five Victoria Crosses won at Arnhem, one should have gone to an RAF Dakota pilot, Flt. Lt. David Lord, for his selfless courage during the resupply operation. Like the other aircrews of 38 and 46 Groups RAF, and the RASC air despatchers who flew with them, he met a storm of anti-aircraft fire unflinchingly, concerned only to support the embattled division below. More than half the aircraft which took part in these missions were damaged or destroyed, and RAF aircrew losses were 21 killed, 159 missing and 12 wounded. The air despatchers suffered more heavily, in percentage terms, than the troops they were supporting: 116 killed and 148 captured out of 900 men. The RAF and RASC were the unsung heroes of British Airborne Forces, and no praise can be too high for men who attempted so much.

Of the other four VCs won at Arnhem two went to The Parachute Regiment: to Capt. Lionel Queripel of 10 Para for a gallant rearguard action

during his battalion's withdrawal to the perimeter; and to Lt. John Grayburn for 'supreme courage, leadership and devotion to duty' despite severe wounds, during the battle at the bridge. Two VCs went to the South Staffords: to L/Sgt. John Baskeyfield, for his single-handed destruction with a 6pdr. anti-tank gun of two German tanks and two SP guns; and to Maj. Robert Cain, for fighting off everything from tanks to flamethrowers, armed first with a PIAT and later, despite his wounds, with a 2in. mortar. Of the five Arnhem VCs, only Cain survived the battle.

Operation 'Varsity': Over the Rhine

In June 1945 the 6th Airborne Div. found themselves at Wismar on the Baltic, having marched on foot from the scene of the last and biggest airborne operation of the entire war.

After Normandy the division had returned to the UK, but were then rushed back to the Continent for a rather grim dose of 'winter leave'—the Battle of the Bulge. They arrived in Belgium on Boxing Day, and spent a cold, uncomfortable month fighting off stiff German attacks and the effects of freezing weather. Fighting for much of the time in white snow-suits, the division went on to capture two villages, Bures and Wavreille, before establishing a firm base on the banks of the Maas near Venlo in northern Germany. In the third week of February the division returned to Salisbury Plain, where they resumed practice for their next—and, they hoped, last—operation, the Rhine crossing.

They did not have long to wait. Operation 'Varsity' took place on 24 March 1945. For this operation the division came under command of Lt. Gen. Matt Ridgway's 18th US Airborne Corps, with Gale as his second in command. Gale had handed over command of 6th Airborne to Maj. Gen. E. L. Bols on 8 December 1944, replacing Browning as GOC 1st Airborne Corps. Browning, affected by the loss of so many of his men at Arnhem, was posted to the Far East to become chief of staff to Mountbatten.

'Varsity' would involve the British 6th and US 17th Airborne Divs.; the latter were going into battle by air for the first time. Like Arnhem, this was to be a daylight operation; but unlike Arnhem, the whole force was to go in at once—and not to form a bridgehead in the enemy's rear, either, but as a 'dramatic extension in depth of a bridgehead already established' (Gen. Hackett's words). The Rhine would first be crossed by Commandos and the 15th (Scottish) Division of British 2nd Army. The airborne force was to seize the high ground overlooking the crossing point—the Diersfordter Wald—only after the 2nd Army had captured the town of Wesel; and then to capture the road and rail bridges over the River Issel at Hamminkeln some eight miles north-east of the bridgehead. This would initially prevent German reinforcements getting to the vulnerable crossing points and, subsequently, allow the Allied spearhead to move east into the heart of Germany.

Shortly after first light on 24 March, 1,348 gliders and 1,696 aircraft carried 21,680 Allied airborne troops to the objective in a single lift. The crews of 38 and 46 Groups, RAF and the USAAF's 9th Troop Carrier Command had the sky to themselves—not a single German aircraft appeared during the fly-in, though several Dakotas and gliders were lost to ground fire. A number of Curtiss C-46 Commandos were also lost. These twin-engined transports had a door on each side of the

Alternative anti-tank weapon available to the paras at Arnhem—if they were very brave, or very desperate, it could be surprisingly effective. The Gammon Bomb, invented by Capt. Arthur Gammon of 1 Para in 1941, was a stockinette bag filled with plastic explosive; the screw cap on top was removed to arm the device, which was then thrown at a tank or bunker.

fuselage, allowing more men to jump more quickly than from the C-47. Despite their many advantages, the Commandos had the disadvantage of bursting into flames at the slightest excuse; and after 22 of them had gone down with their passengers during this operation, they were never used for operational para-drops again. Altogether, 44 transports and 80 gliders were lost on the fly-in.

Supported by every gun available to the 12th Allied Corps on the west bank of the Rhine, and by the guns of the Airborne Corps artillery, the drop went reasonably well. First in were the 3rd Para Bde., who cleared their DZ quickly, and linked up with the ground forces in the Diersfordter Wald later that day after some stiff fighting. Next came the 5th Para Bde., who had a very warm reception indeed. They suffered casualties in the air, and heavier ones on the ground, but succeeded in throwing a screen round the objective to the north and east. The 6th Air-Landing Bde., under Brig. R. H. Bellamy, had the toughest job of all: the capture of Hamminkeln and the bridges. By the time they arrived over the objective there was fog, dust and battle-smoke everywhere; but the *coup de main* parties of (again!) the 2nd 'Ox and Bucks' captured the bridges, while the 12th Devons and 1st RUR

One of the classic Arnhem photos: a 1 Para mortar crew slug it out with II SS Panzer Korps near Oosterbeek church. The near-vertical angle of the tube shows the shortness of the range. (ABF Museum)

took Hamminkeln. By 1100hrs. on D-Day the objective was secured.

The Air-Landing Bde. were helped in their task by the 513th Parachute Infantry of the US 17th Airborne, who had been dropped by mistake on the glider LZ. They made the very best of a bad job, however; and their fighting qualities strengthened even further the close friendship between the American and British airborne troops and their pilots.

The Dash to the Baltic

Two days after the successful airborne operation, the break-out from the bridgehead began. Montgomery (who was by now the Colonel Commandant of The Parachute Regiment) wanted 6th Airborne to spearhead the advance, and this they did, gleefully. Transport was a problem; but, using everything they could lay their hands on, from prams to steamrollers, the division set off in fine fettle. In support were the tanks of the 4th Grenadier Guards and three regiments of artillery, and with this back-up punch the division seemed unstoppable.

Between 26 March and 2 May, Bol's men covered 350 miles—much of it on foot—to arrive in the Baltic port of Wismar just eight hours ahead of the Russians. First in were the 1st Canadian Para Bn., riding on the Guards tanks. Just the day before they had crossed the Elbe. They should not have done: officially, the job was earmarked for the 11th Armoured Div.; but Dempsey, commanding XXX Corps, wanted the honour to go to the 'Red Devils'. Identification problems were solved in true Airborne style when the paras jumped up on the tanks and turned their red berets inside out, showing the black lining. It did not fool anybody into thinking they were 'tankies', but nobody minded, and 6th Airborne led the way. For the 1st Canadian Para Bn.—the only Commonwealth airborne unit—it was a final distinction, adding lustre to a reputation won both in France and at the Rhine crossings. This reputation was highlighted by the VC awarded to Cpl. F. G. Topham, a medic, who had braved shells, machine gun fire and burning petrol while carrying out his duties, though already wounded himself, on the brigade LZ near the Diersfordter Wald.

Three days after arriving at Wismar some of the division moved on: B Coy. of 13th Para Bn. arrived in Copenhagen on 5 May, where they were relieved by the 1st Para Bde. four days later.

For their comrades of the 1st Airborne Div., the period after Arnhem had been one of slow recovery. The 4th Para Bde. had been wiped out; its survivors were posted into the re-formed 1st Para Bde., and the 1st Air-Landing Bde. was also rebuilt. The 1st Polish Ind. Para Bde. remained in the order of battle, and the whole division was slowly brought up to strength.

On 5 May 1945 Urquhart was warned to prepare for an immediate move to Norway. As the Polish Bde. was under orders for a move elsewhere, and his 1st Para Bde. was already en route for Denmark, he had the 1st SAS Bde. pulled back from Germany to join the division. The advance parties flew to Norway on 9 May, the remainder arriving on 13 May. On 26 May, HQ 1st Airborne Div. was redesignated HQ Norway Command, and Urquhart was faced with the monumental task of disarming 35,000 Germans, with only 6,000 Airborne troops to maintain order and prevent sabotage. It was during this period that the division were able to piece together the full story of the ill-fated Operation 'Freshman'; and the bodies of the murdered volunteers were reburied with full military honours.

The 1st Airborne Division was withdrawn to the UK on 26 August 1945, and disbanded in November of that year, almost exactly four years after its formation.

The Far East 1941–46

While the 1st Airborne Div. had been earning its spurs in Europe and North Africa, the Indian Army had created its own airborne forces. On 18 October 1941 the 151st Para Bn. was formed from volunteers serving in the Indian Army and on the Indian sub-continent. Two months later the unit was joined by the 152nd (Indian) and 153rd (Gurkha) Para Bns., and the 50th Indian Para Bde. was formed. The formation HQ and parachute school were at Willingdon Airport, Old Delhi, and the DZ was a race course (whose stands added to the local hazards). At first only two ancient Vickers Valentia biplanes were available, and only 20 or so much-repaired parachutes. A consignment of 'chutes intended for India 'fell off the back of a cargo manifest' in Egypt, and were the basis of Lt. David Stirling's first, and almost fatal experiments with the Special Air Service (see also MAA 116, *The*

Special Air Service). A complete division, with its own aircraft and supporting arms, would eventually come into being in India; but the first use of airborne methods against the Japanese was by 'Special Force'—Wingate's élite Chindits.

Wingate's first Chindit operation was unpopular in some quarters (especially among the Japanese), but he won the confidence of both Churchill and the new Supreme Commander SE Asia, Adm. Lord Louis Mountbatten, and set about planning a second operation for 1944—the most ambitious so far in the Far East war. His secret weapon was to be Philip Cochrane's No. 1 Air Commando, a specially raised formation of the USAAF. They would fly his men in by glider, resupply them by air, and evacuate casualties—this last an important advance over the first Chindit operation, when the wounded had had to be abandoned.

It is no part of the present writer's brief to go into detail on the history of the Chindits, but a few facts tell their own story. Five infantry brigades were flown into three jungle clearings—'Piccadilly', 'Broadway' and 'Chowringhee'—complete with bulldozers, anti-aircraft guns, supporting arms and their heavy equipment, and pack-mules. D-Day was 5 March 1944; and despite many avoidable mistakes (attributable both to Wingate's impatience and his mens' inexperience) a total of six separate brigades were placed deep behind enemy lines over the next few days. Here they sat firmly astride Japanese communications with Burma. When, in June 1944, the exhausted Chindits finally linked up with 'Vinegar Joe' Stilwell's Chinese army, they had crippled three Japanese divisions, demoralised many others, and laid the foundations for 14th Army's eventual stunning victory in Burma. Wingate never saw these fruits of his vision—he had been killed in an air crash on 24 March.

Wingate's theories of air supply were sound and remarkably effective. Put into practice by No. 1 Air Commando, they allowed an audacious plan every chance of success. Many of the lessons learned here were applied—with suitable modifications to take

The last stand: shortly before the withdrawal of the survivors across the river, a paratrooper sights across the verandah of the Hartenstein Hotel with his .30cal. M1 carbine. The ferocity of the battle can be imagined from the fact that Gen. Urquhart's Div.HQ was almost directly beneath this soldier's feet, in the cellar. (Imp.War Museum)

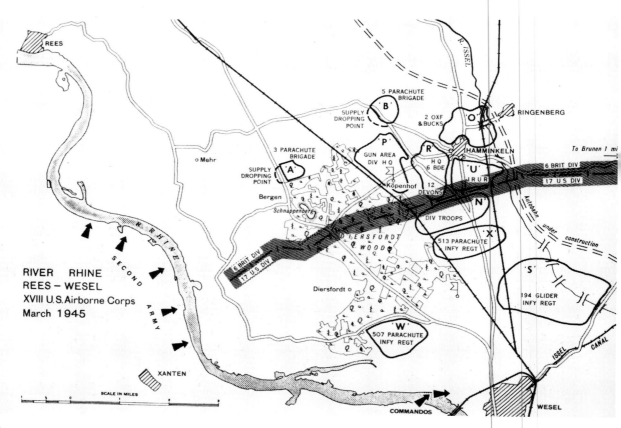

Operation 'Varsity' was a complete success, despite heavy casualties, and the arrival of part of the US 513th Parachute Infantry on the 12th Devons' LZ. The crossings at Wesel and to the north-east of Xanten had already been secured by the time the drop was supposed to go in.

account of terrain differences—to future airborne operations in Europe. As a tiny historical footnote, one may mention that the second Chindit operation saw the first ever operational use of helicopters— No. 1 Air Cdo. recorded 23 resupply, evacuation and communications sorties by the YR-4 two-seater.

As stated above, the 50th Indian Para Bde. had been formed in 1941. This was the nucleus of what later became the 44th Indian Airborne Div., which fought a distinguished war, though mainly in the ground rôle. The Indian and Gurkha troops who formed the bulk of the formation were every inch the equal of the British volunteers; and it was a Gurkha unit which carried out the only major parachute operation of the Far East war, at Elephant Point in Burma.

In 1942 the 50th Indian Para Bde. moved from Delhi to Campbellpur, minus the 151st Bn., which had been transferred to the Middle East to join the

4th Para Bde. and renumbered 156th in the process. Its place in 50th Bde. was taken by the 154th (Gurkha) Para Bn. from the fledgling 77th Para Bde., which was itself replaced by the 1st Bn., The Assam Regiment. With the arrival of Maj. Gen. Down to take command in 1944 there came a major expansion and a general renumbering and reshuffling of units of the new 44th Indian Airborne Division. No. 3 Parachute Training School had been created by this time at Chaklala near Rawalpindi, and it was there that volunteers for the division's 50th and 77th Bdes. reported for training. The 50th Bde. now consisted of the 1st and 4th (Indian) Para Bns., formed from 152nd Bn.; and the 2nd (Gurkha) Para Bn., formerly the 153rd Battalion. The 77th Bde., formed originally round cadres from the 50th, now comprised the 3rd (Gurkha) Para Bn., formerly the 154th; and two new British battalions, built around survivors of the first Chindit operation—15th (King's) and 16th (South Stafford) Para Battalions.

The 14th Air-Landing Bde. was formed from the 2nd Bn., The King's Own Regiment; the 4th Rajputana Rifles; and the 2nd Bn., The Black

1: Cpl., The Parachute Regt., 1943
2: Lt. Col. E. E. Down, 1st Para Bn., 1940-41

A

Arnhem, 1944:
1: Pte., The Parachute Regt.
2: Lt., RAMC
3: Pte., 2nd Bn. South Staffs. Regt.

B

Arnhem, 1944:
1:    Sgt., Glider Pilot Regt.
2:    Bren gunner, 1st Airborne Div.

C

1: Maj. Robert Cain, VC,
2nd South Staffs., 1944

2: Maj. Gen. F. A. M. Browning, 1942

3: Lt. Col. Alistair Pearson,
1st Bn. The Parachute Regt., 1943

4: Maj. John Frost,
2nd Para Bn., 1942

D

See commentaries for individual insignia captions

1 THE LIGHT ARTILLERY

2 1 CANADIAN PARACHUTE BATTALION

3 OXF & BUCKS. Lᵗ INFᵀʸ

4 ROYAL SIGNALS

E

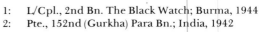

1: L/Cpl., 2nd Bn. The Black Watch; Burma, 1944
2: Pte., 152nd (Gurkha) Para Bn.; India, 1942

153 (Indian) Para Bn.

Indian Airborne Forces

F

1: NCO, Independent Para Sqn., 22 SAS Regt.; Malaya, 1956
2: NCO, 2nd Bn. The Parachute Regt.; Belize, 1983

G

1: Pte., 3rd Bn. The Parachute Regt.; Suez, 1956
2: Pte., 3rd Bn. The Parachute Regt.; Radfan Mts., 1964
3: UNFICYP beret, 1960s

H

Territorial Para Bns., 1984:
1: Sgt., 15th (Scottish V) Bn.
2: Pte., 10th (V) Bn.

I

The Parachute Regt., Ulster, 1970s-80s:
1: Pte., 3rd Bn., South Armagh, 1981
2: Cpl., 1st Bn., Londonderry, 1972
3: L/Cpl., 2nd Bn., 1981

J

1,3: Recruits, P Coy.,
     Aldershot, 1980s
2:   Staff Instructor,
     P Coy.

K

L   1:   Lt., 1st Bn. The Parachute Regt., 1980s   2:   Sgt. PJI, RAF Brize Norton, 1980s

Watch—another ex-Chindit unit. The brigade mustered in November 1944.

All ranks wore the red beret of British Airborne Forces when in barracks (and often elsewhere), and the issue bush hat at other times. They also wore the Pegasus patch and Airborne arm-of-service flash; like the Indian para cap badge, the patch had the word INDIA worked into it, below the horse's fore-hooves. In defiance of regulations most ranks of all units wore their cap badges on a maroon cloth square or diamond on the bush hat.

On 1 May 1945 came the only major parachute operation to be carried out in the Far East: Operation 'Dracula', named after the divisional commander, 'Dracula' Down. This was a battalion-sized assault against Japanese gun positions at the mouth of the Rangoon River at Elephant Point. An improvised battalion group was created from the units of 50th Para Bde., and the drop went in shortly after first light. There was no opposition, and a second lift of supplies and reinforcements went in at 1530hrs. After calling in airstrikes against enemy gunboats and bunkers (and losing 40 casualties themselves to one strike), the paras secured Elephant Point in a final attack with flamethrowers. The next day the unit had the pleasure of watching an Allied amphibious invasion force steaming up-river to Rangoon. 'Dracula' was

FM Montgomery, first Colonel-Commandant of The Parachute Regiment, with senior officers of 6th Airborne Div. shortly after the Ardennes campaign, January 1945. Monty wears the usual two cap-badges—but this time his beret is maroon, and one of them is the Parachute Regiment's. Beside him is the GOC, Maj.Gen. Eric Bols, who took over from the popular Richard Gale just before this campaign. Immediately behind them are the three brigadiers; left to right: Ted Flavell, 6th Air-Lndg.Bde.; James Hill, 3rd Para Bde.; and Nigel Poett, 5th Para Bde. Behind and to right of Hill stands Lt.Col. J. A. Nicklin, popular CO of 1st (Canadian) Para, who was to die on the DZ during the Rhine crossings. (Imp.War Museum)

an unqualified success: one of the few Allied airborne operations of which that could be said, and an ideal example of how a small force should be used in support of a wider strategy.

Later in 1945 the 44th Indian Airborne Div. was redesignated 2nd Indian Airborne Div., and with the new name came a move to Quetta. The end of the war in August 1945 did not bring peace. The division found itself supplying detachments for relief work and counter-insurgency operations as far away as Thailand, French Indo-China and Malaya.

The Indian paras were joined in Malaya by the 5th Para Bde. from the 6th Airborne Div., who had been posted to India to prepare for operations against the Japanese. They arrived in India on 7 August. After an abortive operation in northern Malaya in early September (codenamed, appropriately, 'Fiasco'), the brigade was sent to Singapore, where they spent three months trying to restore

Operation 'Varsity': men of 1st Royal Ulster Rifles from 6th Air-Landing Bde. pose with the road sign marking their objective, secured by 1100 hrs. on 24 March 1945. (Imp.War Museum)

order amid the chaos left by Japanese surrender. Early in December 1945 the situation in Java took a turn for the worse, aggravated by a lack of law and order and of all essential services. The brigade was sent to Batavia and the hinterland in an attempt to improve the situation.

Java was riddled with bandits and nationalist guerillas, who made good use of the ubiquitous jungle; but the paras waded in and, by April 1946, had restored an uneasy peace, while their supporting engineers and medics rebuilt the water and electricity services and created some kind of medical effort. They were helped in this, oddly, by the disarmed Japanese, the only other organised body available; and this unholy alliance handed back an almost 'going concern' to the Dutch in May.

Table 3: 2nd Independent Parachute Brigade Group, 1942–48

4, 5 (Scottish) & 6 (Royal Welch) Para Bns
4/6 Para Bn (1948)
7 Para Bn (from 5th, and to 1st Para Bde, 1946–48)

Under command 300 Air-Lndg.A/T Bty, RA; A Air-Lndg. Lt. Bty, RA: 64 Air-Lndg. Lt. Bty, RA:2 Indep. Para Bde. Gp. Sigs. Sqn; 1 Indep. Glider Pilot Sqn., AAC; 23 Indep. Para Ptn., AAC (Pathfinders); 2 Indep. Para Bde.Gp.Coy, RASC; T Coy, RASC; 751 Para Bde.Coy, RASC; 127 Para Fd.Amb., RAMC; 2 Indep.Para Bde.Gp.Workshop, REME; 2 Indep.Para Bde.Gp.Provo Section, RMP

In 1948 the 2nd Parachute Brigade—as it had then become—was re-designated 16 Independent Parachute Brigade Group; 4/6, 5 and 7 Para Bns were renumbered 1, 2 & 3 Para.

Table 4: Indian Airborne Units, 1941–45

50th Indian Parachute Brigade, 1941–44
151 Para Bn, until 1942, when moved to Palestine to become 156 Para; 152 (Indian) Para Bn; 153 (Gurkha) Para Bn; from 1942, 154 (Gurkha) Para Bn

44th Indian Airborne Division, 1944–45:

50th Indian Parachute Brigade
1 (Indian) Para Bn, ex-cadre 152 Para; 4 (Indian) Para Bn, ex-cadre 152 Para; 2 (Gurkha) Para Bn, ex-153 Para
77th Indian Parachute Brigade
3 (Gurkha) Para Bn, ex-154 Para; 15 (King's) Para Bn; 16 (South Staffords) Para Bn
14th Air-Landing Brigade
2 King's Own Regt, until April '45; 2 Black Watch; 4 Rajputana Rifles; 6/16 Punjab Regt, from April 1945

Post-War Service

For reasons of space, it is impossible to cover the minor operations of the period after 1945 in anything but the most abbreviated form, with occasional digressions:

Palestine 1945–48

1st Airborne Div. was disbanded in November 1945. *6th Airborne Div.* arrived in Gaza, Egypt, from September 1945, ostensibly as Imperial Strategic Reserve, but largely used as security troops in Palestine during a period of illegal activity by Hagana and Palmach, and of outright terrorism by Irgun and 'Stern Gang' (LEHI). The 6th Air-Landing Bde. disbanded, becoming 23rd Ind. Inf. Bde. The division now had *1st Para Bde.* (1, 2 and 17 Para Bns., the last-named disbanded and replaced by 7 Para in 1946); *2nd Para Bde.* (4, 5 and 6 Para); and *3rd Para Bde.* (8 and 9 Para, and 3 Para replacing 1st Canadian Para).

During the division's service in this theatre there were progressive re-organisations. 5th Para Bde. joined it in 1946 but was then disbanded. (12, 13 and 17 Para would all be reformed as Territorial units later.) By early 1948, 3rd Para Bde. had also disappeared, leaving only *1st Para Bde.* (1 Para, amalgamated 2/3 Para, amalgamated 8/9 Para) and *2nd Para Bde.* (amalgamated 4/6 Para, 5 Para, 7 Para). In February 1948 the 2nd Para Bde. was withdrawn from the division and posted to BAOR in Germany. After returning from Palestine to the UK, the division was disbanded in mid-1948.

*   *   *

Only one parachute brigade group was now to remain in the army's Orbat, built around the 2nd Para Bde. in Germany; in July 1948 it was renumbered *16th Independent Para Bde. Gp.*, the '1' and '6' in commemoration of the wartime divisions. In June 1948 the brigade's 5 (Scottish) Para became 2 Para, taking the pale blue lanyard and DZ flash; in July, 4/6 Para became 1 Para, with maroon distinctions; and 7 Para became the new 3 Para, with green distinctions. The brigade returned to the UK in October 1949, to Maida Barracks, Aldershot. (Here they remained until 1968, when The Parachute Regiment HQ moved into the new Browning Barracks, with its battalions and the brigade HQ housed in the new Montgomery Lines n Normandy, Rhine, Bruneval and Arnhem Barracks.) In 1953 the first direct-entry civilian volunteers were accepted, although they had to sign on for three years, rather than the normal two years of National Service; and in 1958 the first direct-entry officers were accepted.

Egypt 1951–54

The brigade arrived in Egypt in mid-October 1951, at a time of unrest, to guard the Canal Zone. At one time it seemed that a full-scale combat drop might be necessary; but in the event the tension produced only sporadic terrorism, particularly around Ismailia, where the brigade was based until mid-1954.

Malaya 1955–57

Between April 1955 and spring 1957 about 80 officers and men, selected from among many more volunteers, formed The Independent Parachute Squadron, 22 SAS Regiment, led by Maj. Dudley Coventry. They were organised and armed as the other SAS squadrons, and performed the same very demanding deep-penetration operations in the jungle country where the Communist terrorists lurked. (For further detail, see MAA 116, *The Special Air Service*, and MAA 132, *The Malayan Campaign 1948–60*.)

Cyprus 1956–58

Between January and July 1956 the brigade arrived on Cyprus, torn by the terrorist campaign of Col. Grivas and his EOKA gunmen, who aimed at forcing Britain to allow a Cypriot union with Greece over the heads of the violently opposed Turkish community. The para battalions took part

in a number of major sweeps, and netted a number of senior EOKA figures, but Grivas himself always escaped capture—though not by many yards, as the display of his jacket, boots and diary in the regimental museum testifies! A highly successful intelligence-gathering operation—'Filter Tip', in

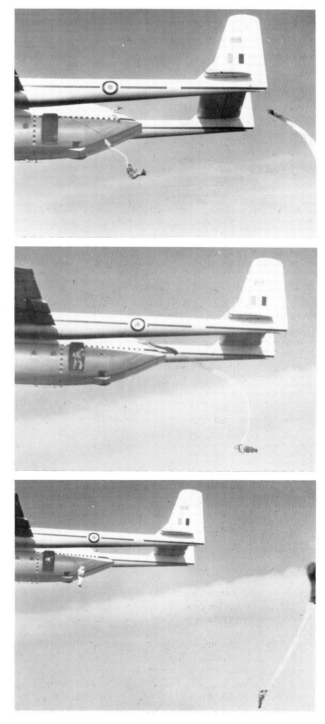

Sequence showing RAF PJIs jumping from an Armstrong Whitworth Argosy C Mk. 1 during trials at Boscombe Down in the 1960s. Initially designed as a civilian transport, the Argosy had to be strengthened to take military loads, and this in turn cut down the load space. It was never used operationally, and had neither the capacity nor the range to be of much value. This sums up perfectly the very serious neglect of Britain's airborne capability during the 1960s and 1970s.
This series shows the opening sequence of the PX1 parachute, which replaced the X-Type early in the 1960s. *Top:* The static line has paid out fully, the inner bag has left the pack, and the rigging lines are beginning to deploy from the inner bag. *Centre:* The rigging lines are fully deployed; the dark canopy is starting to deploy, and will separate from the bag and static line at any moment. *Bottom:* The canopy is clear of the bag, has separated, and is beginning to develop. Twin-boom, high-tail designs allow plenty of room and a clean slipstream for parachutists. (BAe)

Territorial Army paratrooper from 10 Para demonstrates the PX1 Mk. 4 parachute, seen here without the reserve attached. Visible at the front of the harness are the quick-release box, and two pairs of D-rings: the top pair for the reserve, the lower pair for the CSPEP hooks. (Kevin Lyles)

summer 1958—led to the death of Grivas's second-in-command, Matsis, in a gunfight with 1 Para.

Suez 1956

The Anglo-French invasion of Egypt, in collusion with Israel, revealed the shocking state of Britain's so-called Airborne Forces. Tasked to drop on Port Said's El Gamil airfield 24 hours ahead of the seaborne invasion, and supported only by a 'cab rank' of Fleet Air Arm fighters, the 16th Ind. Para Bde. Gp. had available to it barely enough aircraft for a single battalion lift. The Hastings and Valetta aircraft were unable to carry heavy equipment without such expedients as the obsolete and now-rare 'dropping beam' device—one of which was actually commandeered from a museum for use in Operation 'Musketeer'! The new Beverley transports were not yet available, so the brigade

had to leave its new Austin Champ vehicles behind, and scour Cyprus for old jeeps and trailers. The French paras (who dropped a little further south and east) enjoyed, in contrast, a plentiful supply of tail-loading Noratlas and Sahara aircraft, which put anything they wanted on to the ground where and when they wanted it.

At 0415 hrs. on 5 November 1956, 3 Para took off from Cyprus. The drop went in against heavy opposition, but suffered mercifully few casualties. Four hours later the airfield was ready for use; and the next day the seaborne force arrived and linked up, including the rest of the brigade. At midnight on 6 November a cease-fire was announced, and the brigade withdrew to Cyprus a week later.

Jordan, Bahrain, Cyprus: 1958-64

In June 1958 trouble in Lebanon and Iraq took the brigade to Jordan in response to an appeal from King Hussein, at the same time as US forces went into Lebanon. The lack of proper air assets was again underlined: the US paratroopers, in their new C-130 Hercules, could make a round-trip from Germany to Beirut, while the Beverley and Hastings hardly had the legs to take the British paras from Cyprus to Amman and back. The mere presence of the brigade cooled the situation down, however; 1 Para remained in Cyprus as reserve, while 2 and 3 Para guarded Amman airfield, and King Hussein personally. Attached to 3 Para was the brigade pathfinder unit, the Guards Independent Company, The Parachute Regiment.

In 1960 the 'Independent' was removed from the brigade's title. At about this time the 33rd Parachute Light Regt., RA was replaced in the brigade's Orbat by the 7th Para Regt., RHA. The gunners were joined by the Para Sqn., Royal Armoured Corps, whose armoured cars and anti-tank missiles added depth to the brigade's fighting capability. Wearing the RAC's mailed fist cap-badge on their red berets, the troopers manned Ferret vehicles mounting Vigilant AT missiles, and Fox vehicles with Swingfire. There was also some use of the Hornet—basically a Saracen mounting the Australian Malkara AT missile. At a slightly later date the supporting troops of the RCT, RAOC, and REME were re-organised into the 1st Para Logistics Regt., functioning in support of the brigade's fighting units in much the same way as

The PR7 reserve 'chute used today by British Airborne Forces. It has the ripcord mounted on top of the pack rather than at the side—a unique feature. The 22-ft. canopy has a spring extractor; and two gores removed so that, when developed, it tends to 'push' away from the main canopy to avoid potentially fatal entanglements.

today's Commando 'Loggies'.

In 1961 trouble brewed in the Persian Gulf, and within 24 hours of an appeal from Kuwait's ruler, 42 Cdo., RM were on the spot in HMS *Bulwark*. Within 48 hours, some 3,000 British troops were in position, including 2 Para, who flew in from Cyprus without their transport, and commandeered anything that moved to get them to their patrol base at Mutla Ridge some 40 miles from the airport. Inside a week there were 7,000 men in Kuwait: and Iraq lost interest in invading. 'It was', records Maj. G. G. Norton, the regimental historian, 'a notable and bloodless victory for the concept of "Peace-Keeping"'!

By mid-July 2 Para could be withdrawn to Bahrain. From now on all three battalions took it in turns to rotate through Bahrain and the Gulf area from the brigade's UK base; an unpopular posting, it had great political and strategic value.

On Christmas Day 1963 all hell broke loose in Cyprus once again. An independent nation for the past three years, it was still torn by the age-old racial hatreds of Greek and Turk. Recalled from Christmas leave at 24 hours' notice, 1 Para got out

to Cyprus in just 48 hours; and spent an eventful three months trying to keep the two sides apart, and to protect British families in Limassol. Once again, propagandists tried to show the paras in as unflattering a light as possible—not for the first or the last time. To any fair-minded observer, these attempts usually fail: the British 'Tom' is probably his country's best ambassador, being notable for his discipline, common sense, wry humour, and natural sense of justice. He is the ideal 'peace-keeper', as long as nobody takes liberties with his sense of fair play—and if they do, they seldom get a second chance.

On this occasion the British para's impartiality was endorsed when, in March 1964, United Nations Forces in Cyprus took over the British Army's job, with ready British agreement—for UNFICYP was in large part simply 1 Para, exchanging their red berets for the sky-blue of the United Nations. In May the battalion flew home, each man with a UN Medal 'up'—a distinction earned during several further tours in the 1970s by 1 and 3 Para.

Aden and the Radfan: 1964–67

In April 1964, 3 Para under Lt. Col. A. H. Farrar-Hockley ('Farrar the Para') was flown into Aden to take part in operations in the Radfan Mountains to the north against the rebellious Quteibi tribesmen, who were supported by Egypt and the Yemen. The enemy were extremely hardy mountain guerillas, fighting in some of the hottest, harshest terrain in the world. The battalion's B Coy. was first into action, on 3 May at Wadi Tyam, under temporary command of 45 Cdo., RM. The company had an 11-hour approach march and some 19 hours in action, including some brisk exchanges of fire; they named El Naqil village on the lower slopes of 'Cap Badge' as 'Pegasus Village', in modest recognition of their success.

On the night of 18 May the battalion, less B and D Coys., was sent in to secure Bakri Ridge, overlooking the rebel stronghold of Wadi Dhubsan. The non-arrival of naval helicopters left the unit with only two Scout helicopters in support. Nevertheless, Farrar-Hockley pressed on; the men carried some 90lbs apiece, and one company acted as porters for the other, dropping their loads at the top of the ridge and going back down for more while

CSPEP Mk. 2—'Carrying Straps, Personal Equipment, Parachutist'; this device replaced the 'Container, Weapons and Personal Equipment, Parachutist' early in the 1970s. It consists of a wrapping-sheet in which the man's bergen and webbing equipment are parcelled up, with an arrangement of quick-release straps to bind the container together. We are looking at the inner face of the CSPEP, which is worn next to the parachutist's body. The two spring hooks at the top engage with the harness D-rings. The suspension rope, by which the CSPEP is lowered to hang below the soldier during the jump, is clipped through a quick-release device to the lower right leg strap of the harness. The long loop of strap at the bottom passes round the thigh. When the two hooks are released, the leg strap is also released automatically, allowing the container to drop the full extent of the 15-ft. nylon rope.

the other company pressed ahead. By 26 May, supported by occasional air strikes, the force had thrown some of the finest guerillas in the world out of their strongholds among the chaotic rocks of the ridge, leaving only Wadi Dhubsan itself. At first light on that day 3 Para, with X Coy., 45 Cdo. attached, dropped 3,000 feet off the ridge (some of it by abseiling) and went into a full-scale battalion attack with support from mortars, machine guns, artillery and Hunter jets. The CO survived the shooting down of his Scout; and by that night the back of the resistance in the Radfan had been broken.

The final withdrawal from Aden in 1967—a political decision whose dire strategic consequences apparently meant little to the men who took it— took place in a situation of turmoil, as rival nationalist organisations and their outside backers fought over the imminent spoils of independence. 1

Para, sent to Aden in January 1967 to cover the phased withdrawal, had a relatively quiet time— until 25 May, when they moved into the Sheikh Othman quarter, to deny it to terrorists. On 1 June concerted attacks were made by the terrorists on OPs manned by C and D Coys.; the enemy were controlled by loudspeakers in the minaret of a local mosque, but this rather public means of communication enabled D Coy. and some Queen's Dragoon Guards scout cars to hit them hard when they were ordered to change position. More trouble followed the news, five days later, of the 1967 Six-Day War. Lt. Col. M. J. H. Walsh of 1 Para ordered his men back into their OPs, and established himself in 'Fort Walsh', a disused hospital. For some three months the battalion remained in place, meeting attacks with vigour. In late September the unit handed over to the South Arabian Army, and withdrew to a defensive line round Khormaksar airfield until their final departure on 27 November. The unfavourable Press which seems inseparable from these dirty, unpopular post-colonial tasks must be balanced by the decorations awarded: a DSO, an MBE, four MCS, an MM, and 16 Mentions in Despatches, all in some ten months.

Borneo, British Guiana, Anguilla: 1964–69

In December 1964, 2 Para were recalled from Christmas leave and rushed to Singapore in response to Indonesia's threatened invasion of Borneo, part of the newly independent Malaysian federation. Deployed to the border country of Brunei and Borneo after intensive jungle training, the battalion provided its C Coy. for SAS-style training, alongside the Guards Independent Coy and the Gurkha Para Company. Barely a month after arriving, the battalion's C Coy. fought one of the biggest 'battles' of this hard but unobtrusively dispersed war. On 27 April 1965 an Indonesian battalion attacked the company's position before first light, penetrating the forward defences before being thrown back in a hard-fought close-quarter battle. Another company mounted a hot pursuit, and blood-trails were found leading back over the border; but despite intensive patrolling only two other conclusive contacts were recorded. On 29 May one para section ambushed some 40 Indonesians, killing 15 before making off without suffering casualties. A month later a para platoon was compromised at the moment of springing an ambush on 50 Indonesians: ten of the enemy died, but the rest counter-attacked hard, and the paras needed artillery support to withdraw unscathed.

Returning home shortly afterwards, the battalion did not forget the 'SAS requirement'; C Coy. remained the battalion's 'patrol company', the first sub-unit in the brigade to assume this specialist rôle. Today all three battalions have similar companies.

Shortly after this, 3 Para was deployed to British Guiana to keep order in the run-up to independence in February 1966. There was no trouble to speak of; and with huge areas of unpopulated jungle to train in, and local rum at the equivalent of about 20p. a bottle, both officers and 'Toms' enjoyed the tour.

With only Aden, Bahrain and Cyprus left as

Detail of the parachute, reserve, and altimeter used by HALO ('high altitude, low opening') jumpers. Used extensively by the SAS and SBS, the technique is being taught to the Pathfinders of the newly formed 5th Airborne Brigade. The Tactical Assault Parachute Mk. 4 and PR3 reserve are both made by GQ Defence Equipment Ltd.; the PR3 has a side ripcord and a spring extractor. The Irvin Hitefinder is a barometric altimeter device which pulls the ripcord of the main 'chute automatically at about 1,500 ft. (Kevin Lyles)

destinations for foreseeable paratroop deployments, and a shadow hanging over at least two of those, a Socialist government committed to a British withdrawal from 'east of Suez' decided that even one whole brigade of parachutists was an unnecessary burden on the tax-payer. There were many who wanted to see the 16th Para Bde., and even The Parachute Regiment itself, completely disbanded; but even under that government the movement to kill off Airborne Forces was not strong enough. Instead, it was decided in 1968 that only two battalions should remain in the airborne rôle at any time, the third being released for overseas garrison duty; Brigade HQ and the Logistics Regt. would remain in being—but notice had been served that the paras were expendable.

Early in 1969, Anguilla, a minute British colony in the Caribbean, erupted into unrest. This parish-pump quarrel was interpreted by the Wilson government as a major rebellion; and, in what can only have been either a rare and expensive joke, or a ludicrous over-reaction, the government sent in the paras. Briefed to expect an opposed landing, the paras met no resistance. The world's Press was understandably contemptuous; but on the ground, the paras saved the day by striking up a good relationship with the aggrieved islanders. Withdrawn on 14 September 1969, 2 Para was awarded the Wilkinson Sword of Peace for 'acts of humanity and kindness overseas.'

Ulster 1969–19??
There is space here neither for any general discussion of the background and course of the current 'troubles' in Northern Ireland, which broke out in 1969; nor for any detailed description of The Parachute Regiment's service in the province. The bald statistics are simple: 1 Para has served in Ulster six times; 2 Para, eight times; and 3 Para, six times, being the only para battalion not to serve a full 20-month residential tour (as opposed to the standard four-month 'unaccompanied' tour). Casualties include 25 men killed, 16 of them in one incident, at Warrenpoint. Fourteen gallantry decorations have been awarded, including a posthumous George Cross to Sgt. Michael Willets of 3 Para in 1971.

One cannot refer to Ulster service without confronting propaganda, both good and bad. The source of much of the bad has been the main enemy: the Provisional Irish Republican Army (PIRA)— although the regiment has also found itself up against the Marxist Irish National Liberation Army (INLA), and two Protestant terrorist groups, the Ulster Volunteer Force and Ulster Defence Association (UVF and UDA). For the terrorists the red beret is an object of hate and fear second only to the more anonymous image of the SAS. The paras have never had much patience with the kind of abuse and attack to which soldiers are subject in Ulster, and they have always dealt with offenders in a robust way. The one incident which, more than any other, made them an object of fear and respect

An RAF PJI at No. 1 PTS, Brize Norton demonstrates the HALO rig. Here the container is strapped to his backside and his harness, and his weapon is strapped to the container and the left upper arm. British special forces and Pathfinders are currently training in HAHO techniques ('high altitude, high opening'), which exploit the considerable forward vector of modern ram-air 'chutes. Jumping miles away from the DZ with the GQ 360 nine-cell flat ram-air canopy, they will be able to drift in silently over great distances. (Kevin Lyles)

took place in Londonderry on Sunday 30 January 1972—'Bloody Sunday'.

On that day an illegal march by some 3,000 people was joined by some 150 youths, who turned on the security forces with bricks and stolen CS gas canisters. By late afternoon things were getting so serious that 1 Para was ordered to disperse this small group. As they did so, PIRA snipers in the nearby Rossville Flats—and possibly in the crowd itself— opened fire. The men of one platoon returned fire, and in the ensuing exchange 13 people were killed.

The resulting publicity was terribly damaging both to the regiment and to the government. The Lord Chief Justice of the province examined all the charges and the evidence, and cleared the regiment of the charge of opening fire on defenceless and fleeing women and children. The facts are these: that the dead were all young men between 18 and 26; that the paras were returning fire; and that they did not fire indiscriminately—if they had done, the carnage caused by a platoon of men armed with 7.62mm SLRs would have been truly horrific.

Such incidents are almost inevitable in situations where determined and heavily armed terrorists operate under cover of a generally resentful group in the civil population. Where mass civil disobedience and terrorist atrocity occur side by side, the enforcement of the rule of law becomes a trial of endurance, humour, intelligence, and low cunning. The paras have done as much as any unit to uphold and enforce the law, and they have become mightily unpopular for doing so.

On Sunday 27 August 1979 the PIRA scored its only victory of any kind against the paras when a double ambush of Army trucks at Warrenpoint claimed the lives of 16 men of the regiment. On the same day terrorists in Eire assassinated Lord Louis Mountbatten and murdered his young nephew while they were boating on the lough near their holiday home at Mullaghmore.

Since 1972 units of The Parachute Regiment serving in Northern Ireland have been kept well away from the cities, and have been encouraged to use their patrolling skills in the countryside near the border with Eire.

One final word on the public image of the paras in Ulster. The book 'Contact' by Tony Clarke, who had served in Ulster with 3 Para on two tours, was published to a fanfare of Press comment in 1982. It presents a most jaundiced view both of Ulster service, and of the British soldier. One senior NCO who served with Clarke has stated that Clarke's version differs very markedly from the NCO's recollection of the true picture—to put it no stronger . . . A senior officer, speaking off the record, was relieved that the damaging consequences of this very personal view of events and personalities were off-set in the public mind by the splendid performance of 2 and 3 Para in the Falklands War. Truth, as always, was the first casualty in Ulster; and when that happens, it is always the soldier and the civilian—never the political opportunist or the terrorist—who suffers most.

The Diaspora

On 31 March 1977 the 16th Parachute Brigade ceased to exist, killed by financial restraints and political expediency. With the brigade went all the hundreds of men of the supporting arms, essential to the conduct of airborne operations. From that date, only one parachute battalion would remain in the airborne rôle; a second would be 'next-for-rôle'; and the third would be posted somewhere the Army was short of infantry, the three units rotating through these rôles. The airborne battalion ('Parachute Contingency Force') would be the spearhead of 6th Field Force, a new formation tasked with rapid response to threats in the NATO area or to British overseas interests. All three battalions served in Berlin or West Germany at various dates between August 1974 and June 1980. Happily there were no urgent requirements for a 'fire brigade' during these postings, which made a mockery of any plans which might have existed for rapid overseas deployment of a light, strong intervention force.

Wiser counsels prevailed, and in 1980 it was decided that two battalions were needed in the airborne rôle. 1 Para remained with 6th Field Force until 1981, being replaced by 2 Para; and after returning from Germany in June 1980, 3 Para joined 8th Field Force (from January 1982, '5th Infantry Brigade') as its airborne Spearhead unit. In December 1981, 2 Para joined 3 Para; 5th Inf. Bde.'s other unit was the 1st Bn., 7th The Duke of Edinburgh's Own Gurkha Rifles (1/7 GR). Other airborne elements were added to the brigade: 9 Para Fd. Sqn., RE had survived the cuts; and a single Light Gun battery (29 'Corunna' Bty.) from 4th Fd. Regt., RA was trained in the airborne rôle.

After a two-year stint as public duties battalion in Edinburgh, 1 Para were trained in Arctic warfare as part of Britain's contribution to the Allied Command Europe Mobile Force.

The Falklands 1982

In early 1982, Brig. M. J. A. Wilson's new 5th Inf. Bde. still needed a good deal of time to 'shake down' into a wholly efficient and comfortable formation. It was a luxury they were to be denied.

On 2 April 1982 Argentina invaded the Falklands. At that date 1 Para were on an emergency tour in Ulster; 2 Para, the 'Parachute Contingency Force' unit, were deep in preparations for a tour in the jungles of Belize, with both men and equipment dispersed; while 3 Para, the Spearhead battalion, tasked with responding to emergencies at minimum notice, had just been stood down for Easter leave! Somehow the battalion was recalled, prepared, and on board the liner SS *Canberra* by 9 April. At this point 3 Para was under command of the efficient and experienced 3rd Commando Bde., Royal Marines; and it was under this formation that 2 Para was also placed, embarking on the MV *Norland* on 26 April. With them went the rest of the 'PCF': 29 (Corunna) Bty., RA; and the Parachute

Seen from the open boom doors of a C-130 Hercules, men of HQ Coy., 2 Para jump over Salisbury Plain during early 1982. The net skirt round the periphery of the PX1 Mk.4 canopy can just be seen. The rollers on the ramp are for the Wedge Airdrop System, a heavy-load container which is despatched at the start of the run-in over the DZ and followed out by the two sticks of paratroopers. The tendency of the 'Herc's' slipstream to 'suck' the two sticks together—with potentially thrilling results!—can be seen here. (Peter Reilly)

Clearing Troop of 16 Field Ambulance, RAMC—the only regular para-trained medical unit left in the Army. They went equipped for anything; their heavy equipment was stowed on the MV *Europic Ferry*, and was sorted out and 'cross-decked' on the way south.

The landings at San Carlos on 21 May were the usual picture of outwardly chaotic efficiency. 2 Para went ashore by LCU ('Landing Craft Uncomfortable', or 'rubbish skips', to the men) and, after a certain amount of confusion, gained the distinction of being the first major unit ashore at shortly after 0400 hrs. local time. They were met by an SBS beach-marking party, with the words, 'You're not supposed to be here until Monday!' While 2 Para slogged up the dominating Sussex Mountain, 3 Para came ashore from HMS *Intrepid*, engaging in a brief fire-fight with some 40 Argentines, who shot

down two British helicopters before surrendering or withdrawing into the interior. Over the next few days Brig. Julian Thompson's 3 Cdo. Bde. established itself in the beachhead, while the ships offshore withstood constant air attacks. Eventually 2 Para were ordered to prepare a raid against the Argentine airfield and garrison at Darwin and Goose Green; but on 26 May the order was changed to embrace an all-out attack to take the settlements and seal the Task Force's right flank. The battalion's approach to the objective, down a narrow isthmus lacking any ground cover, promised to be difficult; and although enemy strength was reported at a single battalion, 2 Para's CO—Lt. Col. H. Jones, OBE—prepared for the worst. It was as well that he did, since the enemy were heavily reinforced at the last moment.

The attack, against stiff opposition, went in at about 0300 hrs. on 28 May. At about 1200 hrs., A Coy. were held up by a strong enemy position at a point where the enemy were dug in right across the isthmus. Jones went forward to A Coy. with his Tac. HQ, which he subsequently led in a flanking attack

This necessarily small-scale map shows only the main features of the Falklands campaign of May/June 1982, and the considerable cross-country approaches which 2 and 3 Para made—mainly on foot—during the course of their involvement. 2 Para had the dubious distinction of being first ashore at San Carlos—by accident—and the very real distinction of being first into Stanley.

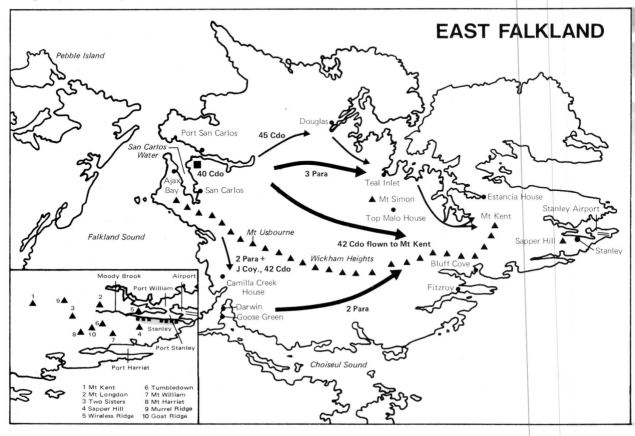

San Carlos, East Falkland, 21 May 1982: 3 Para go ashore at Green Beach 2 in grossly overloaded LCVPs—sitting targets, since they went in later than planned, well after first light. 3 Para had the first contact of the land battle. (MoD)

on an enemy MG position, while ordering A Coy. to assault a strong feature to their front. As he charged the gun position, firing from the hip, he was hit by another MG to his left rear, and died some hours later. His flanking movement both distracted the enemy and inspired his men; if it was madness, it was a divine, Airborne madness, and the enemy position fell 15 minutes later.

Under the second-in-command, Maj. Chris Keeble, 2 Para fought their way down the isthmus; and by nightfall they had taken Darwin and Boca House and had surrounded Goose Green itself. Reinforced that night by a company of Royal Marines, Keeble sent a prisoner over with a surrender demand the next morning. When the Argentines complied, at about 1300 hrs. GMT on 29 May, the paras watched 'gobsmacked' as no less than 1,350 of the enemy lined up to surrender—and another 250 or more were 'not accounted for'. Allowing for the 50 enemy dead and 140 wounded, the paras worked out that they had been fighting at odds of around three-to-one *against*. Their own losses had been 15 dead and 30 wounded.

This first 'real' battle in the regiment's first 'real' war since 1945 caught the imagination of the rest of the Task Force, and the people back home. But when Jones's successor, Lt. Col. David Chaundler, jumped in to replace him a few days later, he was

horrified and furious to discover how little support the paras had enjoyed during their attack. Transport difficulties had meant that only two of the battalion's six 81mm mortars, and very little ammunition, were available. Only three 105mm Light Guns were allocated to 2 Para; and the naval gunfire support hardly materialised: HMS *Arrow*'s single gun broke down during the night battle, and she could not remain on station in daylight.

At first light on 27 May, 3 Para and 45 Cdo., RM set off from San Carlos on an easterly route across the sodden peat and ankle-turning rocks of East Falkland, heading for Douglas and Teal inlet. Lt. Col. Hew Pike's paras took a more direct route than the Marines; they left their bergen rucksacks behind, and marched in fighting order, at a sharp pace. These moves on foot were a notable feature of British operations: helicopters were always in short supply, and those that became available were earmarked for equipment and stores lifts, and casevac. 3 Para reached Teal on 29 May, exhausted but in good heart, and moved quickly on to Estancia House near Mt. Kent, some 15 miles west of Stanley, the ultimate objective. There Thompson

Fitzroy, East Falkland, early June 1982: men of 2 Para re-zero their SLRs on a make-shift range. All wear the Arctic windproof DPM smock and trousers, with either DPM combat caps, or hoods drawn over their conspicuous berets. The foreground man has fitted a compatible LMG magazine to his rifle. The left-hand man has the bracket for an IWS night sight fitted to the top cover of his SLR; and two tracer rounds taped to the butt, for target indication during night battles. (MoD)

ordered them to stop and set up a patrol base.

After Goose Green, 2 Para were lifted by helicopter to Fitzroy; here the arrival of the rest of 5th Inf. Bde. under Brig. Wilson brought the battalion back into the Army, as opposed to the Marine, fold. Taking justifiable risks in his race up the right flank against the time and the weather, Brig. Wilson 'hi-jacked' the one remaining Chinook to get the paras forward fast. But despite hard work, neither the brigade HQ nor the two units drafted in to replace 2 and 3 Para (1st Bn., Welsh Guards and 2nd Bn., Scots Guards) had had the opportunity of working together which alone produces a really tight outfit. On 8 June an Argentine air strike at Fitzroy took out the RFAs *Sir Galahad* and *Sir Tristram*, and most of a company of 1 WG with them. The 5th Inf. Bde.'s planned attacks on the high ground before Stanley were postponed; and 2 Para, having had a chance to dry out in the Fitzroy farm buildings, were ordered back to 3 Cdo. Bde. for the next phase.

The overall plan was for 3 Cdo. Bde. to attack the hill features west of Stanley; 5 Bde. and 2 Para from 3 Bde. would then attack the high ground on the outskirts of the town; and finally, in the event that it was necessary, 3 Bde. would reluctantly assault Stanley itself.

The first phase of the attack went in on the night of 11/12 June: 3 Para's objective was the rocky Mt. Longdon. Led by guides from D (Patrol) Coy., A and B Coys. were to make a pincer attack on the hill's western end, with C Coy. in reserve, and HMS *Glamorgan* giving NGS. A minefield in the path of B Coy. was discovered the hard way by a section commander, and the battle was soon raging; it went on until daybreak. Meeting fierce resistance, the paras had to winkle out the Argentine 7th Inf. Regt. with grenades, 66mm LAW rockets and fixed bayonets. Sgt. Ian McKay took command of his platoon of B Coy. after his officer fell, and destroyed three machine guns with grenades before being killed; he was awarded a posthumous VC. As the night battle wore on, Pike committed C Coy. to the north of A Coy.; and at dawn enemy resistance collapsed. The attack, and subsequent enemy shelling, cost 3 Para a total of 23 dead and 47 wounded.

Back under command of 3 Cdo. Bde. for the second time, 2 Para had remained in reserve for 3 Para's attack on Longdon and 45 Cdo.'s attack on Two Sisters. On the night of 13/14 June the battalion assaulted Wireless Ridge, this time with excellent support: 3 Para's mortars, two full batteries of guns, naval gunfire, and the Scorpion and Scimitar armoured vehicles of a troop from The Blues and Royals. The battle went almost as well as a battle can; and for the first time in the campaign it was the supporting arms which won the engagement, while the infantry cleared the ground and then secured it against counter-attack.

But there was to be no counter-attack: at first light the Argentines could be seen streaming away into Stanley. All ranks, sensing the change in the wind, replaced their helmets with red berets. 'Exploiting forward', A Coy. sprinted off the mountain, and got as far as the race course before being ordered to halt. However, the intrepid Lt. Shaun Webster and Cpl. Owen of D Coy. decided to 'have a look' at Government House, and found themselves being introduced to Brig. Gen. Menendez, who informed them that he would be surrendering at 1600 hrs. that afternoon. The two paras made an excuse, and left . . .

The Parachute Regiment had fought in the British Army's first 'real' war for decades: a hard-fought campaign against an enemy superior in numbers and equipment, dug in on ground of their own choosing. And they had won conclusively, in just over three weeks. Under appalling conditions, the paras had shown that they could still 'hack it' over long periods. For the Royal Marines, too, the campaign was a showpiece. Despite their proven quality and special skills, a chill wind had blown through the Plymouth HQ of Commando Forces at the time of 16th Parachute Brigade's disbandment. For both Airborne and Commandos, the Falklands silenced doubts about the future. Nobody felt more fraternal satisfaction than the Marines when, in October 1983, the Ministry of Defence announced the formation of the 5th Airborne Bde., under Brig. Tony Jeapes, a former CO of 22 SAS. With an airborne formation back in the British Army Orbat (even one which includes an air-landing Gurkha unit), the survival of British Airborne Forces is assured for some time to come.

The Plates

A1: Corporal, The Parachute Regiment, 1943
Emplaning at Ringway, this para wears an X-Type 'chute over the 1943 sleeveless green cotton smock: this had a frontal zip, and press-studs to fasten it between the legs. It is worn over '37 webbing (without, here, the large pack slung round the neck) and the Denison camouflage smock. The 1941 steel helmet has a hard rubber rim (later deleted); this was worn by C Coy., 2nd Para Bn. at Bruneval. The 1941 Airborne-pattern BD trousers have a bellows pocket replacing the patch map pocket on the left thigh. At this date both 'wings' and rank chevrons were, by regulation, to be worn mid-way between elbow and shoulder, and this presentation was therefore common; the 'wings' were later raised to a point two fingers' width below the shoulder seam.

A2: Lt.Col. E. E. Down, 1st Parachute Bn., 1940–41
The 1940 long-sleeved jump smock was patterned on the German version. The helmet is the canvas and sorbo-rubber 'bungee', still seen until the late 1950s. Note the 12ft. 6in. nylon webbing static line, with its forged steel D-ring, neatly stowed in pockets on the back of the X-Type 'chute pack.

Lt.Col. Down wears his webbing equipment under his smock, with the small pack reversed—i.e. slung on his chest. The gasmask container is clipped to the parachute harness on his chest. Note early experimental issue of crêpe-soled high boots, later discontinued as unnecessary.

C Coy., 3 Para, brandish their company flag after marching into Stanley on 14 June 1982, the day of the Argentine surrender. The Parachute Regiment (termed by a senior Royal Marines officer 'a war-winning instrument', in a graceful inter-service compliment) can claim a great deal of the credit for bringing to a speedy and successful conclusion Britain's first conventional campaign since the blighted Suez venture of 1956. In the process they ensured their own survival for the foreseeable future. Incidentally, notice the modest build of most of these men: height gets in the way when leaving an aircraft, weight brings you down faster, and neither is any advantage when crossing country on foot—it is strength and endurance which are all-important. (MoD)

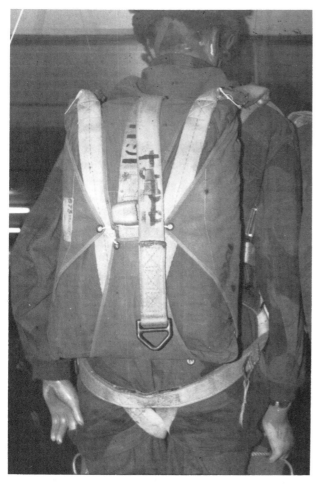

Rear view of the X-Type 'chute, showing static line, outer bag, and two of the four lift webs securing the rigging lines to the parachute harness. Note how the seat strap supports the man's buttocks like a child's swing; the leg straps pass between the thighs, then up and back through the seat strap just below each hip, before passing forward and upward again to the quick-release box.

B1: Private, The Parachute Regiment; Arnhem, 1944
Standard fighting order of steel helmet, Denison smock, Airborne BD trousers (with chamois-lined pockets, and a right thigh knife pocket), 'ammunition boots' and 'anklets, web'. The Sten 9mm submachine gun was widely used, in all its five Marks, by airborne troops, whose requirements had influenced its design; this is the Mk. II model. Note smock cuffs with knit sock-tops sewn on.

B2: Lieutenant, Royal Army Medical Corps; Arnhem, 1944
This wounded officer's smock has been removed, showing features of his BD: the crimson-backed RAMC officer's rank 'pips' on the shoulder straps;

and on the sleeve, the RAMC shoulder title; Pegasus patch of Airborne Forces, and Airborne flash in the same colours of Cambridge blue and claret; and glider badge. Note hilt of Fairbairn-Sykes fighting knife at his right thigh; the leather scabbard with its elastic retaining loop is in the pocket, and the two press studs to fasten the pocket are hidden here by material.

B3: Private, 2nd Bn. The South Staffordshire Regiment; Arnhem, 1944
This soldier of 1st Air-Landing Bde. would normally wear the Denison smock over his BD. The yellow/red shoulder title with integral glider badge was unique in 1st Airborne Div. at this time—other air-landing troops wore the blue-on-khaki glider badge on the right forearm of the BD blouse. He has swapped his Sten with a wounded paratrooper for the latter's Patchett Mk. I SMG; this 9mm weapon, with a 32-round box magazine and a superior effective range of some 200 yards, was currently under trial as a Sten and Thompson replacement, and 100 of them were issued to paras of the division.

C1: Sergeant, Glider Pilot Regiment; Arnhem, 1944
The Denison smock, introduced in 1942, was of green windproof cotton printed with brown and dark green camouflage; the base colour faded to a greenish sand shade. All but the earliest models had a half-length zip; all had storm-cuffs, and could be tightened at the hips by press studs. The tail, which fastened between the legs to stop the smock riding up during a jump, hangs down at the back here— the press studs broke easily. Usually only NCOs wore rank insignia on the smock. This Horsa pilot wears the Second Pilot's glider 'wings' on the left breast: a gold 'G' and circle, supported by pale blue wings. (Earlier, all pilots had worn the Army Air Corps 'wings' with a gold King's crown in the centre; these were later limited to First Pilots.) He carries the .303 Rifle No.4.

C2: Bren gunner, 1st Airborne Division; Arnhem, 1944
This paratrooper wears almost the full set of Airborne fighting equipment. His helmet has early-pattern black leather straps, and is fitted with camouflage netting, scrim and hessian. The camouflage 'face veil' is worn over the shoulders; a toggle rope is worn round the shoulders and waist.

The .303 Bren Mk. I LMG was a most popular weapon, despite its slow rate of fire (450–550 rpm) and the need to carry and re-charge the 30-round box magazines.

D1: Major Robert Cain, VC; 2nd Bn., The South Staffordshire Regiment, 1944

The only Airborne soldier to win the VC at Arnhem and to survive to wear it, Cain wears the South Staffs 'knot' badge on the maroon Airborne Forces beret, and as 'collar dogs' on the 1941 'austerity' No. 2 service dress jacket; note waist pockets cut into the jacket material. The Sam Browne belt has a whistle, whistle-holder and lanyard on the shoulder belt in South Staffs fashion.

D2: Maj.Gen. F. A. M. Browning, DSO, 1942

'Boy' Browning wears the major-general's cap badge on the maroon beret. His Denison smock is of a type adapted for officers, with slanted chest pockets, a wool-lined collar, and a drawstring for tightening—note the eyelets. He wears Army Air Corps wings on the left breast of the smock.

D3: Lt.Col. Alistair Pearson, DSO, MC; 1st Bn. The Parachute Regiment, 1943

One of the lesser-known heroes of Airborne Forces, Pearson was a peacetime Territorial who volunteered for Airborne, and proceeded to win no less than four DSOs and an MC in 18 months, serving with 1st and later with 8th Para Battalion. Between 1 August 1942 and May 1943 the maroon beret bore the Army Air Corps cap badge. The pale khaki 'pip' and crown of this rank are sewn on Airborne Forces' Cambridge blue backing.

D4: Maj. John Frost, MC; 2nd Parachute Bn., 1942

Johnny Frost shortly after the Bruneval raid, which he led, and for which he was awarded the MC. Before August 1942 all ranks in Airborne Forces wore their 'regimentals', and Frost wears the Balmoral bonnet and cap badge of The Cameronians (Scottish Rifles). His 1940 'austerity' BD blouse bears an early Airborne shoulder title; the Pegasus patch;

The quick-release box of a PX1 parachute harness, essentially identical to the wartime X-Type. The harness straps come free when the box is turned clockwise and hit smartly. The breaking strain is 1,500 lbs.

and the yellow 2nd Bn. lanyard, made from parachute rigging line dyed in a solution of Mepacrine anti-malaria tablets[1].

E: Airborne Forces Insignia

(1) Shoulder title, The Light Artillery (2) 1st Canadian Para Bn. (3) 2nd Bn., Oxfordshire & Buckinghamshire Light Infantry (4) Royal Signals. (5) Forearm badge, glider troops (6) Early forearm badge, parachutists; later worn by non-Airborne Forces parachute qualified personnel. (7) 'Unofficial' WW2 RAF PJI badge, upper right sleeve. (8) WW2 epaulette loop, 10th Para Bn.

(9) Cap badge, The Parachute Regt., 1943–52; since 1952 identical but with Queen's crown. (10) Army Air Corps cap badge. (11) British Army parachutist's brevet. (12) AAC pilot's brevet—see commentary Plate C1. (13) WW2 SAS parachutist's brevet. (14) Canadian parachutist's brevet, left breast. (15) Current RAF PJI brevet, left breast.

(16) Current DZ flash, 1 Para (17) 2 Para (18) 3 Para (19) 4(V) Para (20) 10 Para (21) 15 (Scottish V) Para; in WW2, worn as cap badge backing, 5th (Scottish) Para Bn. (22) Regt. HQ, The Parachute Regt. (23) Depot Para (24) 7 Para Regt., RHA (25) 16(L)Coy., 15 (Scottish V) Para (26) 9 Para Sqn., RE.

F1: L/Cpl., 2nd Bn. The Black Watch; Burma, 1944

A ragged jungle veteran of Wingate's brigades, who were air-landed behind Japanese lines, and thereafter operated entirely supported by air. He

[1]Other Lanyard colours worn in 1940–45 included green (1st & 7th Para Bns.); shades of red (3rd & 9th Para Bns.); black (4th & 13th Para Bns.); dark and light blue (8th & 12th Para Bns. respectively); blue/white mixed (22 Indep. Para Coy.)

wears tropical KD shirt and trousers dyed green for the jungle, with a slouch hat and '37 pattern webbing equipment. The weapon is the No. 5 Lee-Enfield jungle carbine, a shorter, handier version of the standard No. 4 rifle used by paras in Europe; the price for convenience was a fearsome kick. Ammunition is also carried in a cotton bandolier with pockets for the five-round clips.

F2: Private, 152nd (Gurkha) Parachute Batallion: India, 1942

On the breast of his KD shirt this Gurkha soldier wears the black-backed Indian Army parachute brevet; on his arm, the white and green flash of the 152nd Bn., and the Airborne title. The Gurkha bush hat, worn here, and the Australian style sometimes worn by other units, often bore a battalion flash on the left side or, after its introduction, the Parachute Regiment cap badge on a square or diamond of maroon cloth. (Inset) the

patches of 153 (Indian) Para Bn., and Indian Airborne Forces.

G1: NCO, The Independent Parachute Squadron, 22 SAS Regt.; Malaya, 1956–57

This NCO, who wears no rank badges, displays what has come to be accepted as 'typical' SAS jungle combat uniform: beaten-up olive green tropical denims, a cut-down olive green bush hat, '44 pattern webbing, and leather and canvas jungle boots (unpopular for falling apart too easily). His 'bergen' is the old canvas type with a steel A-frame, dating from the Second World War. The Winchester 12-gauge pump-gun, with five-round magazine and cut-down barrel, was an excellent close-quarter weapon, even more popular than the prized Australian Owen 9mm SMG for its ability to extract a patrol from an ambush.

G2: NCO, 2nd Bn. The Parachute Regiment; Belize, 1983

This NCO wears the DPM tropical combat suit, with a buttoned fly over the front zipper of the blouse, and drawstrings at waist and ankle. The unpopular British Army jungle boots are replaced by the superior US type. He wears a DPM bush hat and '58 pattern webbing; and carries the M16A1 Armalite rifle. Weighing only 6lbs. and with a 20-round magazine and single-shot or automatic capability, this saw its first British use with the SAS in Malaya, and is still issued for jungle operations.

H1: Private, 3rd Bn. The Parachute Regiment; Suez, 1956

Fresh from anti-terrorist operations in Cyprus, this para wears khaki tropical denims, ammunition boots and puttees, and sand-painted steel helmet. His Denison is of the post-war pattern with a full length zip and elasticated cuffs; its colours differ from the wartime model, with blotches of green and dark brown on a paler drab background. The green 3 Para DZ flash appears on both sleeves, and the parachute brevet on the right shoulder. His webbing is of '44 pattern, without a large pack or

The 1977-pattern DPM Parachutist's Smock. Similar in broad outline to the much-loved Denison, it is now a much lighter and less windproof garment, made in standard British DPM of light green, red-brown, yellow, dark green and black. It has the same bellows pockets with press-studs, full-length zip, knit cuffs, and a fork-piece secured at the back or front with press-studs. Note 1941-pattern parachutist's brevet, above the red-on-black DZ patch of 10 Para. (Kevin Lyles) rucksack; his weapon, the Mk .V Sten SMG.

H2: Private, 3rd Bn. The Parachute Regiment; Radfan Mountains, 1964

This 'Tom' patrolling near 'Pegasus Village' wears KD tropical shirt and trousers, the matching KD bush hat, and '58 pattern webbing belt order—ammunition pouches, two '44 pattern water-bottle carriers, and kidney pouches. He is liberally draped with link for his weapon—as the rest of his patrol would be. It is the 7.62mm General Purpose Machine Gun L7A2, a belt-fed weapon heavier than the Bren but with a higher rate of fire and better sustained fire performance. He would wear only his brevet on the shoulder of this combat uniform.

H3: UNFICYP beret, 1960s

The 1st and 3rd Bns., The Parachute Regiment have each served several times as part of the British contingent of United Nations Forces in Cyprus, each tour bringing them a UN Peace Medal. (The fact that 3 Para had these medals, and 2 Para did not, was the excuse for a fracas of heroic proportions between members of the two fiercely competitive battalions on board the MV *Norland* while returning from the Falklands: conclusive proof that peace had broken out again . . .) The pale blue beret and UN badge are compulsory wear for all UNFICYP troops, and this is the only occasion on which paras can be persuaded to part from their maroon berets.

I1: Sergeant, 15th (Scottish Volunteer) Bn., The Parachute Regiment; 1984

This NCO wears pullover order: heavy duty men's 'woolly pully' with reinforced shoulders and elbows, TMLs, DMS boots and puttees. The rank chevrons and an Assistant Parachute Jumping Instructor's brevet are worn on the sleeve. (The APJI is qualified to take ground or 'synthetic' training sessions, to check 'chutes and equipment before an aircraft descent, and to despatch parachutists from balloons.) His beret badge is backed by a diamond of the Hunting Stewart tartan inherited from the wartime 5th Bn., which is also used as this unit's DZ flash. 15 (SV) Para was formed in 1947 and originally commanded by Lt.Col. Alistair Pearson, DSO, MC.

No. 2 Service Dress, 1982: C/Sgt. Ted Dalton of 4 Coy., 10 Para. White gloves, white belt and sling (both plastic, for easy cleaning), bright 'collar dogs', and scarlet sergeant's sash. C/Sgt. Dalton wears APJI wings; he has also qualified as an APJI with both French and German airborne forces. His father was killed at Arnhem with 1st Bn., The Border Regiment.

I2: Private, 10th (V) Bn., The Parachute Regiment; 1984

He hangs in the PX1 Mk. 5 'flight swing' during Territorial Army training. He wears modern shirtsleeve order: woollen KF shirt ('Shirt, Hairy'); Trousers, Men's Lightweight (TML); DMS rubber-soled boots with puttees; and the maroon regimental stable belt with the cap badge in bold relief on the bright circular buckle. On the left shoulder he wears the maroon and black lanyard of the 10th (Volunteer) Bn., the only battalion not to have been amalgamated or re-numbered since 1944.

The three-point harness of the PX 5 can be seen clearly; the Capewell fasteners at the shoulders have now been modified, to prevent accidental confusion with the steering toggles on the similar harness of the 22-foot steerable parachute—if the Capewells are released in the air, the PX 5 canopy parts company with the harness, with fatal results.

J1: Private, 3rd Bn., The Parachute Regiment; South Armagh, 1981

On a rural patrol, he wears the 1978 DPM parachutist's smock, and the matching cotton trousers—preferred to the synthetic fibre TMLs, which melt and stick to flesh when hit by petrol bomb splashes or tracer rounds. Webbing is '58 pattern, worn with the large Airborne pattern bergen rucksack. High-leg German paratrooper's boots, bought privately, are preferred to DMS boots. Hair is worn longer than normally tolerable, so that the soldier will not be conspicuous when in 'civvies'. His beret, with the black cap badge, is pulled low over the eyes, a regimental affectation which some men think makes them look more sinister. The green lanyard is attached to a compass in the left upper pocket. This GPMG number wears the face veil as a scarf, and brown camouflage cream (made by Max Factor!) on his face.

J2: Corporal, 1st Bn., The Parachute Regiment; Londonderry, 1972

This NCO wears the late-pattern Denison smock (see H1), beret with bright cap badge, and a patrol belt order consisting of two '58 ammunition pouches and a '58 water-bottle carrier. The 9lb. laminated nylon 'flak jacket' is of the early model without non-slip shoulder pads. The 'Northern Ireland' gloves have padded knuckles and fingers (except the trigger finger), allowing him to carry a riot shield comfortably for long periods. The riot stick is standard UK police issue, and is *not* lead-loaded.

J3: Lance-Corporal, 2nd Bn., The Parachute Regiment; Ulster, 1981

Kitted out for a foot patrol in a border village, he wears the DPM para smock, 'OGs' (Olive Green cotton denim trousers), '58 pattern patrol belt order, beret with bright badge, and high-leg 'Northern Ireland' patrol boots: without the need for puttees the soldier can dress more quickly in emergencies, and the boot is easier for medics to cut off in case of injury. The sole is slightly padded, for prolonged wear on hard pavements. The 1974 flak jacket has non-slip shoulder pads for the rifle butt, and the pockets are mounted lower to make room for them. The sling of the L1A1 SLR is attached to his wrist, so that the weapon cannot be snatched in a scuffle.

K1: P Company recruit, Aldershot, 1980s

All recruits must pass through the physical ordeal of P Company before they can go on to parachute training. This recruit is on the 'Shuffle Bars': 40 feet above the ground, he must shuffle along two scaffolding poles ten feet long and two feet apart, stopping half way along to touch his toes and shout his name, rank and number. He wears the red British Army PT shirt with his name stencilled on it; TMLs; and the ballistic parachutist's helmet which

WO1 Bourne, RSM of Depot, The Parachute Regiment and Airborne Forces, in No.2 Dress. He wears the warrant officer's sword and carries a pace-stick. Note subdued 'collar dogs', warrant badge on forearm, and maroon/pale blue lanyard of Depot Para.

was first introduced in 1979.

K2: P Company Staff Instructor, Aldershot, 1980s
Offering words of tender encouragement to a faltering recruit, this typical NCO wears a semi-official sweatshirt in regimental colours with the blue regimental crest and 'Airborne' on the left breast. He wears TMLs, DMS boots and puttees, '58 pattern belt order, and an Airborne bergen—the whole kit weighing some 35 to 40lbs. when ballasted with sand and a full water-bottle.

K3: P Company recruit, Aldershot, 1980s
His pained expression can be put down to the fact that he must cover ten miles on foot in about 1 hour 50 minutes, carrying 30lbs. of kit and an SLR weighing 11lbs.—which has no sling, and must be hand-carried. The DPM cap is worn for the first few weeks; the recruit is then issued with the maroon beret, but wears a green badge backing until he has passed P Company. The General Service DPM smock is worn here, with TMLs with his number-in-course painted on the left thigh pocket; the para smock is not worn until after passing P Company.

L1: Lieutenant, 1st Bn., The Parachute Regiment, 1980s
This officer wears the DPM para smock, TMLs, a 'scrimmed' ballistic helmet, and the high-leg combat boot which replaced the unpopular DMS boot in 1983. His officer's rank 'pips' have the regiment's Cambridge blue backing; he wears the maroon DZ flash of 1 Para on the right sleeve. His main 'chute is the PX1 Mk. 4, his reserve the PR7—the latter introduced in 1981, replacing the old X-Type Reserve Mk. 2, and having a spring-assisted deployment mechanism. As he leaves the door of the C-130 his Mk.1 CSPEP can be seen; the strap is round his right leg, but the two hooks holding the container to his harness are hidden by the PR7, as is the yellow quick-release device attached to the

HRH The Prince of Wales, Colonel-in-Chief of the Parachute Regiment, relaxing with paras after the Bruneval memorial parade of 1982. He wears the stone-coloured summer uniform of a colonel in the regiment, with the gold aiguillettes of an ADC to the Queen. Apart from his Army Air Corps pilot's wings, he also wears—obscured in this photo—his parachute brevet, earned the hard way in 1977.

lower right leg strap of the 'chute harness, from which the container will dangle when he releases it.

L2: Sergeant PJI, No. 1 PTS, RAF Brize Norton, 1980s
RAF Parachute Jumping Instructors, who are all sergeants or above, can be the most loved or most hated men in the world for paratroopers. This PJI wears an olive green aircrew flying suit, with his name and PJI brevet on a cloth patch sewn to the left breast; rubber-soled PJI boots; white leather aircrew gloves are obscured here. His 'chute is the Irvin Instructor's Model, with a manual ripcord on the left side of the harness. The broad web belt with two buckles is a safety harness, incorporating a friction shock absorber to slow his fall if he slips out of the aircraft.

Notes sur les planches en couleur

A1 Il porte le parachute *X-Type* par dessus la veste sans manches 1943 '*Jacket, Parachutist*', par dessus la blouse *Denison*, par dessus son equipement a sangles. Notez la poche de jambe spéciale du pantalon et le rebord en caoutchouc du casque, caractéristique de courte durée. Notez la combinaison bizarre de chevrons de rang et du *brevet* de parachutiste. **A2** Blouse à manches longues modèle 1940 original. Le casque de formation fut vu de temps en temps jusqu'aux années 1950.

B1 Parachutiste 'typique' de 1944. **B2** Les insignes de manche sont le nom du *Royal Army Medical Corps*, l'insigne '*Pégasus*' des *Airborne Forces* et la barrette rouge et bleue indique également qu'il appartient à des troupes aéroportées; et l'insigne des planeurs. **B3** Ce type d'insigne d'épaule appartenait exclusivement à ce bataillon. Il porte l'une des cent sous-mitrailleuses Patchett utilisées expérimentalement à Arnhem.

C1 Remarquez le *brevet* de co-pilote sur le côté gauche de la poitrine. **C2** Remarquez le 'voile de visage' porté sur l'épaule et la '*toggle rope*', article utile d'emploi général.

D1 Ce soldat, seul survivant d'Arnhem décoré de la VC porte les caractéristiques régimentales de l'uniforme des *South Staffords*, avec un béret rouge. **D2** Remarquez l'insigne de général de division sur le béret et le *brevet* de pilote *AAC* sur la poitrine. **D3** Insigne de chapeau de *Army Air Corps* porté sur le béret rouge entre août 1942 et mai 1943. **D4** Coiffe du régiment des *Cameronians*, encore portée par cet officier en 1942; notez aussi la fourragère jaune du *2nd Para Bn*. à cette date.

E Voir les légendes en anglais pour reconnaître les insignes.

F1 Les vêtements et l'équipement sont ceux qui sont distribués à l'infanterie pour la jungle; aucun article spécial 'aéroporté' n'était utilisé par ces troupes en Birmanie. **F2** Notez *brevet* à support noir de parachutiste de l'Armée de l'Inde et l'écusson vert et blanc de ce bataillon. En médaillon: l'écusson de *153 (Indian) Para Bn*.; et l'insigne '*Pégasus*', modèle Armée de l'Inde.

G1 Aucun insigne n'était porté pour les patrouilles de jungle et l'équipement est improvisé à partir de n'importe quels articles pratiques des modèles 1944 et 1958; le sac à dos date de la deuxième guerre mondiale. La '*pump gun*' Winchester était populaire pour le combat de près sur un terrain de jungle. **G2** Uniforme tropical *DPM* actuel, avec équipement à sangles du modèle 1958 et fusil M-16 américain.

H1 Notez le modèle après-guerre de la blouse Denison, avec *DZ flash* vert des *3rd Para*. Un uniforme tropical léger et un casque peint de couleur sable sont portés, avec un équipement de modèle 1944. **H2** Uniforme tropical et équipement 1958, à part la gourde de modèle 1944. Le *brevet* de parachutiste est le seul insigne porté durant le combat. **H3** Le seul chapeau pour lequel les *paras* ont jamais abandonné leur célèbre béret rouge.

I1 Uniforme avec chandail en laine et caractéristiques du bataillon de cette unité écossaise. Notez le *brevet* spécial de *APJI*—instructeur adjoint de saut. **I2** Uniforme de caserne moderne typique, avec la fourragère du bataillon et la '*stable belt*' du régiment. Le harnais de formation est le Mk.5 PX1.

J1 Il porte la blouse moderne de parachutiste *DPM* avec pantalon assorti, un équipement de modèle 1958, un grand sac pour troupes aériennes et des bottes de parachutiste allemandes acquises personnellement. Cette longueur de cheveux n'est tolérée que parce qu'elle permet au soldat de ne pas se faire remarquer lorsqu'il est en civil dans cette zone hostile. **J2** Le dernier modèle de la véritable blouse *Denison* était encore porté au début des années 1970—ici, avec la '*flak jacket*' et l'équipement personnel léger typiques pour le service de la sécurité urbaine. **J3** La nouvelle blouse *DPM* est portée avec la '*flak jacket*' plus moderne de 1974 qui a des tampons anti-glissants sur les épaules.

K1 Pour la formation physique, le soldat porte cette chemise rouge, sur laquelle est marqué son nom. Le casque de parachutiste est le modèle 1979. Cette recrue se balance à 13 mètres du sol durant la formation au parachutage. **K2** Tenue typique d'un instructeur accompagnant les recrues dans leur formation; le sac contient 20 kilos de sable. **K3** La recrue, qui n'est pas encore autorisée à porter le béret rouge, doit parcourir 16 kilomètres en moins de deux heures, en portant environ 20 kilos d'équipement. L'uniforme *DPM* de 'service général' est porté—la blouse de parachutiste est également interdite tant que la recrue n'a pas passé les épreuves initiales.

L1 Prêt à sauter d'un C-130, cet officier porte le parachute Mk. 4 PX1, le parachute de réserve PR7 et le conteneur d'équipement Mk. 1 CSPEP attaché à la jambe, ainsi que le sac à dos des troupes aériennes. Les insignes du rang sont sur fond bleu clair régimental. Le '*DZ flash*' est de couleur marron rouge, qui est la couleur du *1 Para*. **L2** Cet instructeur de parachutage de la RAF porte un harnais de sécurité pour l'empêcher de tomber de l'avion et un parachute léger commandé manuellement en cas qu'il le fasse.

Farbtafeln

A1 Dieser Soldat trägt über seiner ärmellosen '*Jacket, Parachutist*' von 1943, über seinem *Denison*-Smock und über seinen Gurten einen *X-Type*-Fallschirm. Beachten Sie die besonderen Hosenbeintaschen sowie den Gummirand am Helm der nur kurze Zeit verwendet wurde. Achten Sie auf die merkwürdige Kombination des Rangwinkels und des Fallschirmjäger-*Brevets*. **A2** Ein langärmeliger Original-Smock aus dem Jahre 1940. Bis in die 50er Jahre sah man gelegentlich diesen Trainingshelm.

B1 Ein typischer Fallschirmjäger aus dem Jahre 1944. **B2** Die Armelinsignien bestehen aus dem Titel *Royal Army Medical Corps*, dem '*Pegasus*'-Abzeichen der *Airborne Forces* und dem rot-blauen Streifen, und dem Luftlandetruppen-Abzeichen. **B3** Nur dieses Bataillon trug diese Art von Schulterinsignien. Er trägt eines der 100 Patchett-Maschinenpistolen, die bei Arnhem ausprobiert wurden.

C1 Beachten Sie das *Brevet* des Kopiloten auf der linken Brust. **C2** Achten Sie den 'Gesichtsschleier' über den Schultern sowie auf die '*toggle rope*', ein sehr nützlicher und vielseitiger Gegenstand.

D1 Dieser einzige, überlebende VC-Sieger von Arnhem trägt die Regimentsabzeichen der *South Staffords*-Uniform sowie die rote Felduniformmütze. **D2** Achten Sie auf die Abzeichen des Generalmajors an der Mütze sowie auf das *Brevet* des *AAC*-Piloten auf seiner Brust. **D3** Zwischen August 1942 und Mai 1943 trug man dieses Mützenabzeichen des *Army Air Corps* und der roten Felduniformmütze. **D4** Dieser Offizier trug 1942 noch die regimentsübliche Kopfbekleidung der *Cameronians*. Achten Sie auf die damals übliche gelbe Schnur des *2nd Para Bn*.

E Erläuterungen der Insignien finden Sie in englischer Sprache.

F1 Uniform und Ausrüstung für die Dschungel-Infanterie. Diese in Burma eingeflogenen Truppen trugen keine speziellen Abzeichen der Luftlandetruppen. **F2** Beachten Sie das schwarz gefütterte Fallschirmjäger-*Brevet* der Indischen Armee sowie das weiss-grün Tuchabzeichen dieses Bataillons. Auf dem eingesetzten Bild sehen Sie das Tuchabzeichen 153 (Indischen) Fallschirm-Btl. und '*Pegasus*'-Abzeichen, Indischen Armee.

G1 Dschungel-Spähtrupps trugen keine Insignien, und ihre Ausrüstung bestand aus Gegenständen aus den Jahren 1944 und 1958. Der Rucksack stammt aus dem Zweiten Weltkrieg. Das Winchester-'*Pump-Gun*' war beim Dschungel-Nahkampf sehr beliebt. **G2** Gegenwärtige *DPM*-Tropenuniform mit Ausrüstung aus dem Jahre 1958 und einem amerikanischen M-16-Gewehr.

H1 Beachten Sie den Denison-Smock aus der Nachkriegszeit mit dem grünen '*DZ Flash*' der *3 Para*. Der Soldat trägt eine Tropen uniform und einen sandfarbenen Helm sowie eine Ausrüstung aus dem Jahre 1944. **H2** Tropenuniform und Ausrüstung aus dem Jahre 1958 mit Ausnahme der Feldflasche von 1944. Das einzigen Insignien im Einsatz ist das Fallschirmjäger-*Brevet*. **H3** Die einzige Kopfbedeckung, für die die *Paras* jemals ihre hochgeschätzte rote Felduniformmützen aufgaben.

I1 Eine ähnliche Uniform mit Wollpullover und Bataillonsabzeichen dieser schottischen Einheit. Beachten Sie das besondere *Brevet* des *APJI*—stellvertretender Fallschirmspringlehrer. **I2** Typische, moderne Kasernenuniform mit Bataillonsgurt und '*Stable belt*' des Regiments. Das training-Gurtwerk ist ein PX1 Mk. 5.

J1 Er trägt den modernen *DPM*-Smock der Fallschirmjäger mit passender Hose und eine Ausrüstung von 1958 sowie den grossen Rucksack der Luftlandetruppen und Stiefel der deutschen Fallschirmjäger, die er privat gekauft hat. Der Soldat darf sein Haar nur deshalb so lang tragen, damit er in Zivilkleidung in dieser feindlichen Gegend nicht auffällt. **J2** Die letzte Ausführung des *Denison*-Smock wurde noch Anfang der 70er Jahre getragen—hier sehen Sie ihn mit der '*Flak jacket*' und leichter, persönlicher Ausrüstung, die für den Stadtdienst typisch ist. **J3** Der neue *DPM*-Smock mit der später ausgegebenen '*Flak jacket*' (1974), die an den Schultern mit gleitsicherem Stoff besetzt ist.

K1 Beim Körpertraining tragen Soldaten dieses rote Hemd, auf dem der jeweilige Name markiert ist. Der Helm des Fallschirmjägers stammt aus dem Jahre 1979. Dieser Rekrut balanciert während seines Vorbereitungstrainings für Fallschirmjäger in 13 m Höhe. **K2** Typische Kleidung eines Ausbilders, der das Training mit den Rekruten mitmacht. Im Rucksack befinden sich ca. 20 kg Sand. **K3** Der Rekrut darf die rote Felduniformmütze noch nicht tragen. Er muss in weniger als zwei Stunden eine ca. 20 kg schwere Ausrüstung 16 km weit tragen. Er trägt die allgemeine *DPM*-Uniform. Auch den Fallschirmjäger-Smock darf der Rekrut erst tragen, wenn er den Grundkurs bestanden hat.

L1 Dieser Offizier trägt einen Fallschirm der Art PX1 Mk. 4 und bereitet sich auf den Sprung aus einer C-130 vor. Ausserdem trägt er einen Reservefallschirm der Art PR7 und einen Mk. 1 CSPEP-Behälter, der am Bein festgebunden ist, sowie der hellblauen Regimentsfarbe zu sehen. Das '*DZ flash*' hat die kastanienbraune Farbe der *1 Para*. **L2** Dieser Fallschirmjäger-Ausbilder der RAF trägt Sicherheitsgurte, damit er nicht aus dem Flugzeug fallen kann, sowie einen leichten, manuell bedienten Fallschirm, falls es doch passiert.